Being John Lennon

[signature]

DAYS IN THE LIFE

OF

Sgt PEPPER'S
ONLY DART BOARD BAND

Being John Lennon

DAYS IN THE LIFE

OF

S^{GT} PEPPER'S ONLY DART BOARD BAND

Martin Dimery

First published in 2002 by SAF Publishing Ltd
under the PopTomes imprint.

SAF Publishing Ltd
Unit 7, Shaftesbury Centre, 85 Barlby Road,
London. W10 6BN, ENGLAND

www.safpublishing.com

ISBN 0 946719 43 8

Front cover painting: Michael Cole
Back cover and spine photos: Julie Withers

Printed in England by:
The Cromwell Press, Trowbridge, Wiltshire.

Introduction

I've heard tribute artists talking earnestly, in reverential tones, about the acts they choose to plagiarise. This suggests they are in some way living out their own fantasies through the act, hiding behind a more glamorous persona than themselves. It's a kind of applied Celebrity Obsession Disorder. I suppose it stops some of them lurking around on doorsteps waiting to gun down their object of obsession.

Perhaps, on reading this diary, you may decide the writer suffers similar delusions. If so, I can assure you that you are mistaken – and if you persist in this absurd assumption... I shall be waiting.

So, having got that out of the way, I'd like to do the honourable thing and thank those who have helped me indulge my pretence at being John Lennon. Firstly, to my wife Anne and our children, Tom, Richard and Olivia: I know it must be embarrassing for you.

Next, my mum Pauline; her sister Denise; my brothers Paul and Hugh; Paul and Cheryl Price and other members of my family and friends who have indulged my need to dress up in a satin frock-coat and wig: The therapy is working well, so thank you.

Finally, to my best mates and fellow inmates in Sgt Pepper's Only Dart Board Band: Paul McCoatoff; Rolf Harrison; Gringo Barr and Sgt Pepper; alias John Freeman; Lester Mason; Stuart Berry and Robert Waller. I hope you too manage to recover. And thanks to those who were successfully released from the asylum: Mike Walker, Steve Hurd, Alex Hurd and Tony Stockley.

Oh, and not forgetting The Beatles: You may wish to sue – but I am assured, you do not have a leg to stand on.

And what better way to open our tale than with a quote from the world's other greatest rock band... The Who:

"I have to be careful not to preach
I can't pretend that I can teach
And yet I've lived your future out
By pounding stages like a clown.
And on the dance floor broken glass
The bloody faces slowly pass
The numbered seats in empty rows
It all belongs to me, you know."

From "The Punk and The Godfather"
by Pete Townshend.

From the album *Quadrophenia*.

January

January 1ˢᵗ - 2 a.m

Most of the audience has sloped off into the night to vomit and urinate over ornate thresholds throughout the normally sedate streets of Bradford-on-Avon. Depressingly sober, we stagger under the weight of amplifiers and drums to awaiting estate cars, smiling benignly at semi-comatose well-wishers.

"Great gig, lads" one of them slurs in the direction of guitarists Alex and Steve. Myself, one of the "front men" in the line-up, he fails to recognise. This is quite usual, although in this instance temporary amnesia and partial blindness after fifteen pints of "Old Profanity" may have played a part. I am only ever recognised if members of the audience happen upon me pre-show, in the gents, back brushing a shoulder-length wig and applying make-up. If there is anything more potentially embarrassing or dangerous than this, it has yet to be invented.

I first impersonated John Lennon when I was young enough to rely on my own hair. That was in the stage show *A Beatle Remembers* which did the rounds in the mid-eighties. Since then, a West Country production of *Tommy* led to the formation of Who Two and turned me into a Roger Daltrey doppelganger.

The Who, as we discovered, appealed to a hard-core of loyalists, comprising throwback teenage converts and middle-aged Mods. Nearly all were male, still claiming "The

Kids are Alright" but less enthusiastic about dying prematurely. Who Two gigs generated more testosterone than a stud farm in Spring. The atmosphere could be threatening but euphoric, every show a flat-out, twelve-round contest.

After two punch-drunk years with the "Pinball Wizard", a new theatre project called *All You Need is Love* featuring the music of The Beatles came along and it was decided to swap "Substitute" for "She Loves You" and Shepherd's Bush for "Strawberry Fields".

Last night's audience was fairly typical of any attending a performance by Sgt Pepper's Only Dart Board Band. Certainly there was a more agreeable mix of the sexes but The Riverside is a venue that seems to attract a younger clientele. A slightly rowdy reception greeted our delayed arrival onstage, caused by the non-appearance of guitarist, Lester Mason. Lester and family were due to return from holiday in good time to get to the gig. He duly phoned to confirm the good news that the plane had indeed arrived on schedule. The bad news was that his Volvo had proved less reliable than the plane and had engineered an extension to his sightseeing trip. He now had ample time to partake of an in-depth study of the landscape Cardiff Airport's car park.

Sgt Pepper's Only Dart Board Band has evolved to incorporate eight members including Beatle "lookalikes" up front. One advantage of this is the ability to reproduce (without the use of much-despised backing tapes) the more complex Pepper-period arrangements. Another advantage is flexibility, in that we can usually cover for company absences. With Rob Waller and his magnificent organ pre-booked to play "Quando Quando" in a club somewhere, and vocalist Mike Walker otherwise engaged in a Highland Hogmanay orgy, we were for once, heavily dependent on the normally reliable Lester.

Frantically re-arranging the set-list backstage, the supporting DJ covered the hiatus with the kind of heavy-handed irony guaranteed to have an audience baying for our blood from the outset. Not daring to increase the delay, we brazenly took to the stage with a loose but loud rendition of "Sgt Pepper's Lonely Hearts Club Band", in the hope that the volume of musical output, coupled with the volume of alcohol intake, would coerce the audience to a positive response. We were right.

Lester, whose holiday tan had already been reduced to a pale shadow, arrived almost in time to greet the New Year, and fortunately with the best part of the set still to play.

Time and again we have discovered that young audiences revere the music of The Beatles as much as their elders. The narcotic numbers go down particularly well. By the end of the night various Lucy's, if not in the sky, were certainly up on the tables – with Diamond Whites.

January 1ˢᵗ

Ears ringing. Headache. Throat like an amateur sword swallower. "I'm too old for this," I complain. My wife Anne agrees. What does she know?

January 2ⁿᵈ

Comfort shopping in the local record emporium called Raves from the Grave. Sounds like it should be the probable name for my next band. They have more old vinyl in stock than an MFI warehouse. Displayed in the blues section, I chance upon a rarity by the legendary Champion Jack Dupree. How is it all old or dead blues players acquire the epithet "legendary"? A bit like knighthoods for Senior Civil Servants, I suppose. I resolve to inform Steve Hurd our "legendary" bassist of the aforementioned album entitled *Blues from the Gutter*.

Steve's main claim to fame is that he toured with Champion Jack when the legendary man uprooted himself from the gutter and moved from Mississippi to a mortgaged bungalow in Mansfield... or somewhere. Anyway, Steve can quietly boast an appearance with Jack on the late sixties and early seventies German TV show *Beat Club*. Trouble is, he was flown in and out of Bremen without ever seeing his own youthful, and no doubt smouldering, TV persona. During our last visit to Germany, a close friend, Heinz Becker, played us his personal video archive of *Beat Club* shows, but Steve remained elusive throughout.

Dave Dee of "Zabadak" fame, made sure that his own contributions to *Beat Club* were preserved for posterity by purchasing the rights to the series. Having failed to turn up in the Becker collection, Steve's quest for the elusive tape came to an abrupt end recently when he received an unexpected phone call at work.

"Hello, Dave Dee here mate. Got no record of your *Beat Club* gig. Sorry."

Resisting the temptation to enquire as to the well-being of Dozy, Beaky, Mick and Titch, Steve politely thanked Mr. Dee and allowed him to return to "Xanadu" and his fine collection of whips.

January 3rd

Good news! Kath at the Black Swan confirms that our January 9th booking is back on. Following a previous appearance by our combo, the Environmental Health Deparment has now lifted the ban. Something to do with the new double-glazing. We can only hope to God they haven't fitted a decibel limiter. These devious devices cut all power to the amps the moment anyone ventures over a prescribed volume. Last encountered at our Bishop's Stortford bash, this sinister suppresser of pleasure tripped out on no more than a lightly tapped tambourine. Who Two would have blown the bastard up.

January 5th

Publicity day. This involves lengthy hours spent licking envelopes containing promotional material. We have a healthy number of bookings for this year, but too many pub gigs. Most bands, ourselves included, have contrived to hand the average pub fee back over the bar before they've even finished the soundcheck. Of course, finding quality bookings is supposed to be the purpose of the show-biz agent. In reality, representation by an agent involves little more than having your details stuffed in a filing cabinet at an office over a chip shop in Dorking. Agents rarely know much about the acts they're representing, resulting on one disastrous occasion with Who Two being promoted as a country and western duo.

Agents still manage to squeeze out the best deals, so one is reluctant to offend them. John Freeman, our irrepressibly satirical answer to Paul McCartney, almost broke this unwritten rule.

Approached after a particularly exhausting performance with the request, "I'd like to represent you. Who's your agent?" "Well, unless I'm mistaken... *you* are." John replied whilst trying half-heartedly not to look too smug.

Amongst the client-list of one of the agencies "representing" us are no fewer than 150 tribute bands of which at least nine others impersonate The Beatles. Acts that catch the eye are those who appear not to take themselves too seriously like "Closet Queen", "Phil Haley and his Comments" or "Fred Zepplin". Elvis impersonators dominate the list of great pretenders, along with Abba. Some of these acts are no more than singers accompanied by half an hour's worth of pre-recorded tapes. In the case of Spice Girls lookalikes it's hard to imagine an act that lasts much more than ten minutes. A decent Abba tribute show featuring live band, full beards, flares and hot pants are quoted in the region of

£1,500 per night. Not the kind of fee, I hasten to add, that we might expect for playing at the Black Swan.

January 6th
Big gig offered at a RAF base. Officer's mess, no less. None of your common-or-garden NCOs. Make myself a mental note: Must stop Freeman learning Lennon's "Working Class Hero".

January 7th
Back to the day job. Commuting along the idiosyncratic highways of Somerset. Nowhere en-route is it more difficult to navigate, particularly in Winter, than the village of Pilton with its tight bends, pot-holes and slippery inclines. The nearest railway station to the village is about ten miles away and the bus service as predictable as a stag night with Liam Gallagher.

Those who say that only an optimist, idealist or an idiot would attempt to organise anything more than a bring-and-buy sale in Pilton, are simply tempting someone like Michael Eavis to turn it into the world's largest camp-site.

Last year's Glastonbury Festival was bigger than ever, and five members of the band were initially delighted to be in the Pilton programme. Appearing in a new musical, based this time around on the songs (but not the life) of The Kinks, called *Waterloo Sunset,* Glastonbury was set to be the highlight of the tour, a landmark in our respective careers. Performing on an open stage in a cow field and knee-high in something resembling the effluent from a colonic irriga-tion kit, reduced the glamour of the occasion somewhat. In addition, bellowing the dialogue to the accompaniment of police helicopters flying overhead proved a tad problematic.

Certainly the subtlety of the quieter scenes wasn't exactly enhanced by the percussive sound effects of steel hammers on tubular aluminum, courtesy of some particularly insensitive scaffolders. Add to the equation the drifting noise from the world's largest amplification system and you will gather that the more intense moments of *Waterloo Sunset* were mostly wasted – unless a party of hearing impaired lip-readers happened to be in the vicinity. And who was it that had the cheek to be broadcasting so loudly in our direction from the main stage? None other than Ray Davies himself, thanking us all for the "Days" – one of several songs pulled out of the musical at short notice, following the breakdown of eighteen months negotiation for permission rights. Our second performance of the play was in the much more accommodating theatre marquee, by which time drummer Tony Stockley had extricated his badly battered, expensively hired camper-van from "The Healing Field", and was available to help counteract other extraneous sounds.

Passing through Pilton reminded me of how wonderful it was to get back to being The Beatles; to do away with any semblance of artistic pretension, dress up as our all-time heroes and steal their act note for note. For which audacious purpose, we need acquire no specific permission whatsoever.

So, as the drumrolls and fanfares of the New Year fade; on behalf of one of the burgeoning battalions of bastard Beatles, I would like to propose a toast to John and Paul. May your music live forever... or, at least until after Friday night at The Black Swan.

January 15ᵗʰ

The Black Swan is a homely, Victorian pub close to the town centre of Trowbridge. It stands at the end of a row of two-up two-down terraced houses designed for the loyal servants of the renowned sausage factory nearby. Trowbridge is famous for its pork pies and little else. Despite being the county town of Wiltshire, the place has about as much night-life as the isolation ward of a geriatric hospital. Hence local factory workers find amusement and pleasure (legend has it) in adding their own ingredients to the pork pie production... ingredients, it would be safe to say, that are unlikely to find their way into *Delia Smith's Guide to Healthy Eating*.

Kath and Charlie are an unprepossessing Cockney couple nearing retirement age. At first glimpse, Charlie appears to be the kind of landlord likely to complain about the volume before the band has even plugged in. But contrary to first impressions, Charlie and Kath have been great patrons to many local bands and have helped the Dart Board Band build a loyal following at the Black Swan. Tonight, however, we learn that Charlie and Kath are selling up and moving on, which gives the gig something of an edge.

The ever-so-salubrious "dressing room" at the Swan is a room above the outside toilets. It is accessible by an exterior staircase which, at this time of year, is usually coated with a film of ice. As John, Mike and I descend the staircase, view impeded by long fringes and sunglasses in the pitch dark, we all manage to slip at least once before careering through the back entrance and into the lounge bar. Familiar faces line the walls, seemingly enraptured by our walk-on to the repeated opening riff of "Sgt Pepper's Lonely Hearts Club Band". Not many bands take the trouble to dress up in Trowbridge. The pub is relatively small and our eight piece line-up barely fits onto the makeshift stage at the end of the L-shaped lounge. We squeeze through the tightly-packed audience and step up to the microphones, Steve signals to the rest of band, the introduction is rounded off by Tony's brief drum roll, I take a deep breath and hope to God my voice can faithfully reproduce the note locked in my head: "It was twenty years ago today"... So far, so good.

John, myself and Mike introduce ourselves as the surviving Beatles: "Paul Lemmon", "John McCarthy" ("formerly with the Beirut Beatles") and "Bingo Card" ("otherwise known as The Fat Controller"). It's the same old gags, same old slightly patronising laughter. The carefully rehearsed ad-libs between songs are gradually becoming a little more slick. Best laugh of the night however is provided courtesy of Rob "Silver Fingers" Waller (or "Broken Fingers" as I call him in the script). Rob, having not played at the last gig, was decidedly rusty on his harpsichord-like run-downs between verses on "Strawberry Fields". Rob adamantly insisted on including these little trills when we realised that we had somehow omitted them when originally learning the song.

For this rendition, he cocked up the sequence between third and fourth verses with such amazing ineptitude that every note of the nine was a "bummer". Audible sniggers from the band broke into guffaws of laughter when Freeman announced over the music: "and on keyboards... Mr. Les Dawson." I giggled girlishly through the rest of the song which we passed off as an accurate rendition of the *Anthology* version. Rob's blushes were in part, spared by the fact that he was completely invisible to the audience, standing behind a loudspeaker and sandwiched somewhere between the pool table and, appropriately enough, the dart board.

Among our regulars is a disabled guy on crutches who always sits on the same stool at the bar. He looks possibly thirty, with a slightly unkempt beard, gold rimmed glasses and smokes roll-ups. Even though he arrives early when there are few punters in the pub, he never tries to make conversation, seeming distant and self-conscious. As the night wears on, I always look to see if he is swaying on his stool and singing along. It is a kind of bench-mark. The earlier he sings, the better we are playing. By the time we reach "All You Need is Love" near the end of the set, he is usually weeping into his beer. Tonight the tears begin on "Hey Jude". We were obviously on form... or maybe he's just had a bad week.

After the gig Alex announces his impending retirement from the band. This is not unexpected. Alex is Steve's son. He joined the band to play guitar on the show *All You Need is Love* which spawned Sgt Pepper's Only Dart Board Band. As the show was performed mostly by students at Frome Community College, Alex didn't seem out of place. Furthermore, he is a tremendous guitarist with great prospects. I think we were all a bit surprised that he wanted to tag along with the old man and his middle-aged chums once *All You Need is Love* had finished, but as he said, "It's better than working at Sainsbury's, even if the money's not so good." It's a useful analogy. Music business glamour is to the local band what Sainsbury's is to a corner shop. That makes us the musical equivalent of a Happy Shopper, I suppose; cheap, cheerful and convenient. I don't think I want to dwell on that one.

Anyway, Alex is off to university in September and has 'A' Levels to consider, so he will make a gradual and tactical withdrawal. We have already considered this eventuality and despite my offer to switch to rhythm guitar and let Lester loose on the lead breaks, it is decided that Rob can easily double up when not playing keyboards. This frequent spurning of my (some say) "unique" guitar skills is beginning to rankle.

January 30th

Sgt Pepper's Only Dart Board Band prides itself on being completely self-contained and needing neither to work with, or act as, a support band. Of course, this is an entirely unjustified and egotistical form of artistic snobbery – but when performing with a tribute band, you need all the artistic snobbery you can get. Naturally, the offer of a significant financial inducement to support another band can lubricate like honey when it comes to swallowing the cod liver oil of pride.

Tonight we play second fiddle, guitar and drums to a Rolling Stones tribute aptly entitled Stoned Again. The occasion is a fund-raiser for a school in Keynsham near Bristol. The school PTA promote several rock nights every year, taking big financial risks on "name" acts and in the process turn the school hall into a passable and popular cabaret club.

We arrive early to find Stoned Again's hired PA already set up. Either side of this modest school stage stand two enormous stacks of loudspeakers. Someone had presumably told Stoned Again they were playing Keynsham's answer to Wembley Arena. Next to theirs, our nifty PA combo resembles a 1970s Ferguson hi-fi system.

Following the soundcheck we head for the bar, awaiting the arrival of our eminent headliners who have phoned in to announce a hold-up. We have to decide which numbers to omit from our normal set. Reducing the act from two-and-a-quarter hours is not easy given The Beatles' prolific output. We all pitch in with personal preferences: Steve doesn't like "Lovely Rita" presumably because of the bass line. Rob is desperate not to repeat his keyboard nightmare on "Strawberry Fields", John wants to keep in "Revolution" because he's finally learned the words – and while everyone else is heartily indifferent to the obscure "Hey Bulldog", Mike is reluctant to lose the one opportunity afforded by the set to extemporise on his convincing interpretation of a barking dog.

The tetchy atmosphere is suddenly broken by the interruption of a distinct Brummie accent: "Allo. You the uther band?"

"Yeah", we reply, looking up with a degree of suspicion.

"Great! Oi'm Malcolm from Stowned Agin. Sorry we're late."

Malcolm is a leather-jacketed thirty-something with shortish, well-groomed, curly hair. A slight craggyness and a gen-erous mouth hint at which Stone Malcolm might be.

"We've 'ad a noightmare on the rowd. Bloody van caught fire outside Sainsbury's in the bloody petrol station! I runs into the kiosk, I say, "'Ey, mate? Yow got a fire extinguisher? Me van's on fire!" And yow know what? He hadn't bloody got one! There's a burning bloody van standing by one of their pumps and he didn't bat an eyelid! It's a wonder Oi'm still here to tell the tale. If it wasn't for the fact a geezer in a Merc had one in his boot, 'alf of Bristol would've gone oop in flames! Anyway, you soundchecked alright?"

"Yeah, fine thanks," says John.

"Beatles, are yow? We've done a few with Beatles tributes. We did an outdoor thingy last summer with er... that famous lot... yow know..."

"The Bootleg Beatles?"

"Yeah. Good gig."

"So, which one are you then?" Mike asks with less than convincing sincerity.

"Me? Oi'm the singer... Mick Jagger," says Malcolm, as if we might have been under the impression that the Stones' front man was Charlie Watts.

We are then joined by two more "Stones". Both are lean and crow-like, wearing long coats and scarves, spray-on trou-sers and pointed boots. Each lodges a cigarette on his bottom lip, closing one eyelid against the resultant drift. It is impos-sible to tell which was Keef and which was Ronnie, but that rather added to the authenticity. The Midlands accents seem laughably incongruous and I secretly hope they'll use them in the act.

A large audience, a short set and the likely comparisons between the two bands get the adrenaline and the bowels flowing. It is hoped the pungent aroma, reminiscent of an E.U. surplus brussel sprout warehouse, dissipates before

Keynsham's young ladies reclaim their hockey changing room on Monday morning. We decide to keep three recently added numbers in the set; "Drive My Car", "Lady Madonna" and "Hello Goodbye" all of which go down well and sustain the musical momentum. Any band doing a half-decent set of Beatles songs is going to be a hard act to follow, even for a Stones tribute. I find myself smugly wondering what Stoned Again are thinking as I catch sight of them standing in the shadows at the back of the hall.

Rapidly striking the set, there is just time to grab a pint before heading back to spend the night together with their satanic majesties. The four instrumentalists launch into the grinding chords of "Start Me Up" and the audience awaits in anticipation the arrival of Mick (a.k.a. Malcolm) Jagger. Suddenly, he appears... bodice waistcoat, silk trousers and long scarf, circa Knebworth 1976... claps his hands in circular fashion, jumps up and down and breaks into that familiar, hip shaking strut of the little red rooster. Offstage, Malcolm has donned a long wig, eye shadow and expertly expanded his lips with make-up. The effect is startling. Malcolm *is* Mick. Only in profile can the distinction be made. Something about Malcolm's emerging double chin isn't quite right.

The Wembley Arena PA is disappointingly dull and lacks the gritty, dirty sound associated with the Rolling Stones. Despite this, Malcolm's getting into the "South London – wish I was born born in Memphis – grammar school drawl" with no residual Dudleyisms and the boys look and sound the business. They're being paid a lot more than us, but after the agent's cut, the cost of the PA hire, the hiring of the now-cremated van and petrol costs from the Midlands, the take-home difference is no more than the price of a take-away on the long road back. It's difficult to tell which of us got the greater satisfaction.

The Idiot's Guide to the
Songs of The Beatles

By now dear reader, many of you are undoubtedly considering the possibility of forming a Beatles tribute band yourself in the time honoured "if that lot can do it, so can I"
tradition. Whether to assist embryonic tribute bands or to
help those readers who insist on imposing their saloon bar
musical opinions on any poor sod lonely enough to listen; I
would like to bestow a few handy hints and observations on
the works of Lennon and McCartney. Much of my knowledge and expertise has been gained from several years of dis-
secting, analysing and generally buggering up The Beatles.

To begin with, let us consider a song mentioned in the
previous chapter. Other examples will follow in due course:

The Idiot's Guide... No: 1
Strawberry Fields

This song should not be attempted by chronic amnesiacs. The words make no sense at all and are full of contradictions. For example: "No one I think is in my tree, I mean it must be high or low" ...and the rhymes tend to disappear halfway through. Consider the following lines... "That is you know you can't tune in but it's all right. That is I think it's not too bad".

Authenticity can be achieved when reproducing this song on stage by smoking marijuana or getting very, very drunk prior to performance. Indeed Lester Mason, our George, has perfected an excellent club singer version of "Strawberry Fields" in a style parodied by Billy Connolly.

To achieve this effect take a large brandy in one hand, a panatela cigar in the other (having first loosened your bow tie) and annunciate the opening line in a slow drawl as follows: "Ler me tek yeowww dahwnnnah, Cows h'I'm geowen teoowah, Stro'bry feols."

The "Stro'bry" in "Stro'bry feols" should be delivered in

short, clipped, poor-man's Frank Sinatra style. You can try this version at home.

If utilising a keyboard synthesiser to duplicate mellotron or harpsichord sounds, always ensure your instrumentalist is hidden from view of the audience (preferably squeezed between the pool table and the dart board) and do not laugh when he enters in the wrong key.

"Strawberry Fields" is of course a masterpiece of production. Listen to the anthology version with Lennon playing alone on guitar and then hear the final cut. The dream-like stillness of the song is realised by slowing down the tape and commencing with a chorus, while strings punctuate the melody in a low, brooding fashion. This cleverly avoids the usual treacle effect of pop song orchestration and is a great example of the intuitive genius of George Martin. The Dart Board Band played a simplified arrangement of the song reasonably well but it's hard to do "Strawberry Fields" justice live and we eventually dropped it from the set.

There – my application for the post of music critic on *The Times* is in the post.

February

February 1st - Let me take you down

Admitting to the day job is never easy. Especially after a gig. People have a tendency to ask whether we really do this for a living or do we have 'real' jobs? It is then I wish I could say: "Yeah, I'm actually a session musician..." or maybe: "a script-writer," or even: "a Consultant Gynaecologist". Telling them, "I'm a teacher", conjures images of all those amateur talent shows and operatic societies propped up by schoolteachers with far more confidence than capability.

Having developed an interest in youth drama from a spell in the National Youth Theatre, I decided upon a career in either teaching or acting. After four years studying Drama at Middlesex Polytechnic, I made a two-pronged attack on both possible professions. Despite appearing in London fringe theatre shows and being offered work in a professional production of *Joseph and His Multi-Coloured Raincoat*, I was denied entry to the actors union Equity after three applications, for no discernible reason. This was during the days when it was easier for a Communist to join the Masons than for a suitably experienced degree-trained performer to break into show-biz.

I was then offered a job interview at a new community school on the Isle of Wight. Medina High School was just reaching the end of its building programme prior to the swingeing public spending cuts of the late seventies. If we thought it was bad then, we hadn't anticipated the arrival of Mrs Thatcher.

Medina was a wonderfully designed and equipped comprehensive school, though architecturally not dissimilar to a waste re-processing plant on an industrial estate. It was officially opened in 1981 by (a no doubt horrified) Prince Charles.

The Medina Theatre was very much underplayed in the job description. On the day of the interview, the other candidates and myself were casually led through the dining room by the Head of English to what we expected to be a school hall. We entered at the rear of the stalls looking down on a steeply raked fan-shaped auditorium containing 420 seats, to an open amphitheatre-type stage. There was a collective gasp. My mind was made up.

I was appointed later that day as assistant to the Theatre Director and Head of Drama, Ray Thomas. Apart from being a dynamic Drama teacher, Ray turned out to be a hell of a good drummer with whom I had my first real experience of playing in a rock band.

The Equity experience had however, left an aftertaste as bitter as consuming a bag of under-ripe lemons. Risking a permanent blacklisting, I wrote two fairly vitriolic letters to *The Stage* newspaper accusing Equity of conspiring to keep young performers out of the business. This drew predictable denials from the Membership Secretary suggesting that "Equity was encouraging new talent". He resigned a few years later for encouraging prospective female members to personally parade their talents in his bedroom.

Four years on, I finally obtained my Equity card. By then, Anne and I had decided to uproot ourselves from the idyllic island and with five month old Thomas in tow, settle in Frome, Somerset. Our commitments were then too great for me to sacrifice the slave-like but steady salary afforded by teaching.

Frome College it was, that lured me to Somerset. The school's Merlin Theatre was even better established than Medina's and inevitably I became heavily involved in productions and administration, at one point having to run the theatre and teach full time. Twelve years and almost as many nervous breakdowns later, I managed to leap over the wire and flee the pursuing hounds to arrive in the neutral territory of Millfield School.

Millfield is to education in Somerset what Switzerland was to the rest of Europe during the War; a land-locked island of peace, privilege, elegance and wealth. The school is among the richest in the world with facilities and resources of which State school teachers can only dream. If they ever find time to sleep, that is. It is not unusual at Millfield to find oneself confronting the type of child who, were we in his country not mine, could summarily demand my execution for failing to return his "prep" on time. Indian and Arabian princes rub shoulders with the sons of Russian politicians and the elegant daughters of racing drivers and rock stars. It is not unknown to teach a lesson in the sure knowledge that one forgetful clip round the ear would instantly invoke (through the skylight) the arrival of Boris junior's bodyguard, thus risking a return to Cold War hostilities.

Today, in the Millfield car park, I spotted a "celebrity parent" with whom I was itching to recount the "Stoned Again" episode. Rolling Stones fans might well remember the promising career of Chris Jagger, Mick's younger brother. Chris released a noteworthy debut album; appeared in a number of stage shows and acted on TV, but has inevitably developed his career in the insurmountable shadow of Jagger Major. Chris now writes frequently for national newspapers and performs with a couple of bands, one of which, Atcha

Acoustic specialises in a wonderful blend of Cajun and blues played by some top session men. They have a good following in Germany and Scandinavia where they tour frequently and manage to flog quite a few albums of fine songs, mostly penned by Chris. Watching "Stoned Again" reminded me of how much Mick Jagger had grown to be a knowing parody of his onstage persona. Chris, by contrast, has the talent and sincerity that Mick might have retained if he'd been a little less of an icon.

As I cross the car park, a battered old VW estate (by far the worst car of any Millfield parent) pulls up beside me. "Martin... alright? How yer doin'?" The voice is familiarly Jagger-esque. The face peering out of the window breaks into a smile drawing back heavy lips that wreathe seemingly bountiful teeth. The Jagger genes course through the family. Chris's boy, Robert, the rapscallion of the Remove, is a taller carbon copy. Chris turns up the car stereo.

"It's me new album. You like it? Cost a bloody fortune in studio time."

"Got a recording deal?" I ask him.

"No. You don't know anyone do you?"

He is entirely oblivious to the irony. I answer politely in the negative.

"How's Robert doing? Handing in all his work is he?"

"Not bad. Tries hard on the bits he enjoys."

"Yeah, right. Been doing much with The Beatles, then?" he says, with smirk.

"Not bad for the time of year."

"Know any good places locally?"

"Not that pay well."

"Yeah. They're all bloody cheapskates round 'ere. Still, I'll try and get over to see your lot sometime. I've seen that other lot...the whatsits...The Bootleg Beatles... at some big do. I was standing next to George Harrison at the time. He kept complaining about them playing the wrong chords."

I manage to engineer the conversation around to Stoned Again. Trouble is, half way through the story I started to wonder if he really wants to hear all this. After all, it's about Mick again, isn't it? The poor sod must get fed up to his admirable back teeth of listening to stories about The Stones. I decide to play down my Malcolm Jagger impersonation and change the subject. We agree to have a pint sometime.

Chris has been decidedly nice since he came loitering up the school drive one morning and accosted me for a gig in the school's Meyer Theatre which, as well as teaching a virtually full timetable and coaching the fourth eleven football team, I also happen to manage. Despite an appallingly low turnout from pupils and public alike, Atcha Acoustic did a very professional job and I offered them three consecutive Monday nights last summer in Millfield's "Holiday Village". This is when the school magically transforms into what can best be described as "Butlin's for Stamp Collectors". Chris could only do one of the dates, but his piano player, Ben Waters, took on the other two nights with his Boogie Band. Ben, who recently recorded with Ray Davies (a songwriter I worship, albeit reluctantly for reasons earlier described), has just (according to Chris) been asked to audition for McCartney's latest album. And this is the bloke who told me he'd fill in if we "needed someone to dep on keyboards".

Perhaps I'll give him a ring sometime:

"Er...Ben? Martin Dimery here from Sgt Pepper's Only Dart Board Band. Do you think you could put McCartney on hold today? Only Rob's hurt his hand playing that tricky run-down in "Strawberry Fields" and we need someone to stand in tonight in Trowbridge. I'm sure Sir Paul won't mind. There's twenty quid in it plus a free pint. ...Oh, and er... can you provide your own costume?"

February 5th

Phone call: (Cockney wide-boy accent).

"'Allo, Mickey here from Camden Town Gigs. Laaaved your video mate. Yeah, we can do that booking on May 2nd at the West One Four Club. Saaanday lunchtime was it? Where you playing the night before? Cranfield University? Where's that? Oh, Luton way? Never 'eard of it. Mind you, we do a lot of universities, don't we? Could get you on the circuit. I've been looking for a Beatles tribute for some time. We promote at some of the top venues in Laaandan; Dingwall's, The Dublin Castle...you name it... Yeah... ...yeah... Well, Mawtin, as far as maaaanay goes, I'm seeing this as a try aht, alright? I mean, we ain't seen you perform and I'm looking to spend a lot of dosh on the venue, ten thaaasand flyers, ads in the papers an' that... so, I'm probably running a loss on it... baaaat... on the avver 'and, once we've seen yer, we could do some good staaaf wiv yer in the universities an' that. Then we're talking good maaaanay... Eh? ...Yeah, alright. You're twisting my arm. Go on then. I'll give you a ton for your trouble... a hundred nicker, alright? As long as you don't mind me inviting a few gorgeous women down to pose abaht wiv yer. Only I've got a arrangement wiv the *Daily Sport*. You'll get some good publicity aht of it!"

I agree to the deal. My euphoria at breaking into the London scene swiftly passes as the front page of the *Daily Sport* comes to mind, the headline announcing:

Why Don't We Do It In The Road!

"But I always do it in a wig," says pervy Public School Sir, 42."

February 12th

Today's General Studies lecture in the theatre features the annual visit to Millfield by Mike Hurst. Mike was a member of The Springfields at the height of their fame. It has long been forgotten that The Springfields were the first British act to reach number one in the American charts, before Dusty Springfield pitched her husky bar-room blues vocals as a solo artiste. Before the show, Mike privately reveals that Dusty is now terminally ill.

Mike's lecture is far from being the reminiscences of a sad, old, fading pop-star who once touched glory. He has continued writing and producing to the present day and is a fascinating authority on the development of popular music. This is a subject I have often assumed I knew a great deal about – until I heard Hurst's lecture-demonstration. Singing and playing his way through songs that sank without trace in 16th century England to resurface in the19th century Mississippi Delta, he is a witty and engaging raconteur, making an excellent stooge of young Robert Jagger to whom he was introduced before the show. Robert sat alone in the front row to hear his illustrious uncle Mick being described in the terms of a 1960s *Daily Express* editorial. The family similarities were hilariously apparent to a school audience, most of whom are barely old enough to be married to a Rolling Stone. I meet up with Mike afterwards and he tells me how difficult he is finding it to launch a commercial tour of his show. I am strangely re-assured by this. Here is a man who actually topped the bill on which The Beatles played a supporting role and he is finding it harder than us to get gigs. It transpires he's heard of our tribute show which gives me an unexpected buzz. On the other hand maybe he was just being polite. Mike is writing a book on the development of popular music and is talking with a TV company about a documentary. I hope his plans come to fruition. His natural modesty and charm are deserving of success.

4 p.m

Sense of elation as half term arrives.

The drive home is a rare pleasure compared to the black, bleak, evenings of just three weeks ago. Arriving in Frome during daylight encourages me to call in at the scene of tomorrow night's engagement: The Cheese and Grain Hall.

This bizarre sounding building was renovated in the middle of last year to provide a home for indoor markets, social events and performances. Naturally, this has upset the area's other arts institutions which could do with a little less competition in a market town of only 23,000 people.

I discover on my visit to the hall that ticket sales are low. Despite the success of our last show, we may be mistaken in returning so soon. In addition, the hall has lost its novelty value. Audiences at the excellent monthly comedy nights for example, are starting to fall significantly.

Having accepted a 20% pay cut to help out the troubled management, it looks like we might just as well have played a local pub for two hundred quid. I am spotted by the hall manager who invites me into her office. As with our previous engagement, she has failed to give us a contract confirming the arrangement, despite reminders. She brightly informs me that they have now "sorted out" the precise contractual details for all future acts, based on a box office split and she promises to bring the contract in before the show. "The new contract," she continues, "which will apply to every band using the hall, ensures that the booking is a *shared* venture in every respect. This means we *share* the hiring fee of two hundred and fifty pounds plus VAT and then we *share* the Performing Rights fee, these are deducted from the top, so to speak, then we *share* the profit 50-50."

I am aghast.

"You mean you are asking us, in effect, to hire the hall and then give you half the proceeds?"

"No. The hiring fee comes off the top. It is *shared.*"

She is now becoming assertive to the point of eyes bulging and lips drawn back across her teeth as if ready to attack the nearest available limb.

Being John Lennon

I genuinely wonder if I have taken the wrong inference. Of course, the hall cannot hire itself to itself, so in effect she has decided to charge us a hiring fee on top of taking half our profits. This is the kind of deal of which Don King would be proud. I suggest that it's rather unfortunate that, having failed to deliver a contract, she now leaves it until the night before the concert to inform me that she is breaking the original arrangement. She then becomes increasingly agitated accusing me of trying to "rip them off" and showing resentment at the size of fee our last promotion brought in. I remind her of our considerable costs at which point she launches into a long tirade cataloguing all her overheads right down to the loo rolls. I allow this seizure to simmer, give a slight pause and with all the smugness of Tony Blair on election night, remind her that, "I am, in fact, a theatre manager." Analogies of grandmothers and the ancient art of egg sucking become superfluous.

She finally agrees "to waive the hiring fee on this occasion" with a slightly hurt benevolence suggesting an act of unparalleled generosity. I stand to leave, almost overwhelmed by the urge to stick her Cheese and Grain where it would most quickly turn rancid but resist the temptation, recognising that she is angling for a cancellation.

Not wishing to give her the satisfaction, with a brief, "Well, thank-you for *sharing* that with me," I depart.

February 13th
About a hundred turn up to the Cheese and Grain. Despite the hostile atmosphere from the management, we give the full works. One or two members of the audience ask if we're disappointed by the turn-out. This provides the ideal cue for my "I once played in front of an audience of one" anecdote, but frankly it's too boring to repeat.

The Cheese and Grain manager's recommendation that

we go elsewhere for our next local engagement, will be taken up with enthusiasm.

February 18th

Flying visit to Luton. Anne's dad Dick is recovering well from recent operation. The kids are particularly fond of their grandad and we've not told them that for the last two years he's been battling prostate cancer. The treatment has come on in leaps and bounds since my own father eventually succumbed to the same illness six years ago and to-date he has kept up a busy and fulfilled schedule.

For many years Anne's dad was a drummer in a dance trio, proving very popular at functions in the Luton and Bedford area. Dick will be the first to admit he was hardly Bedfordshire's answer to Buddy Rich but his engaging style and the ability get a party going helped fill a diary that was the envy of many more serious rivals. He is clearly in his element now that our youngest, Olivia, has taken up the drums at the age of ten. Olivia who's normally quite shy and reticent has brought along her sticks and practice pad to show off her technique. She's being taught by Tony Stockley, the Sgt Pepper drummer, who also happens to co-write the exercise books most kids use when taking their grade exams. This gives Dick ample opportunity to issue some instruction born of experience.

There's nothing Dick enjoys more than offering advice. In the past he has offered me advice on many subjects. Two that most readily spring to mind are the art of making a pot of tea (in the manner recommended by self-styled "tea-making experts," no less); and the special technique involved in slicing a tomato:

"You don't want to do it like that... see, that's how to slice a tomato. That's how your top chefs do the job."

He is however, a much loved personality who managed to entertain the entire ward and secure invitations to all their

Being John Lennon

houses on his departure from hospital. Delving into his DIY video collection back home, he produced an informative film on drumming techniques that Tom, Richard and Olivia watched with gratifying interest. I was slightly discomfited though, by their similar absorption to a video on the art of wood turning.

February 19th

Return home to find a message on the answerphone:

(Cockney wide-boy accent) "'Allo, Mawtin, Mickey 'ere, "Camden Tahn Gigs." Sorry mate. New management at the West One Four Club. They're dropping everything after the end of April. As you're May 2nd, I've 'ad to cancel. Give us a ring some time."

And so the quest to crack "Laaandan" continues. Well, strike me pink. Still, I didn't much fancy snuggling up to an over-exposed model in the *Daily Sport* anyway.

Should you be in doubt, that last sentiment was a flagrant untruth.

February 20th

No gig tonight. While it's good to have a Saturday off, the day lacks focus. Normally I work Saturday mornings and if there's a fourth eleven match, spend much of the afternoon running around a football pitch dressed in black and blowing a whistle in declamatory, theatrical fashion.

Lounging about the house somewhat restlessly, I suddenly remember we haven't collected the poster boards advertising the Cheese and Grain show from assorted railings around town. Given that the boards are expensive to produce and likely to provoke the threat of prosecution for illegal fly-posting, I begin my tour of recovery.

Frome town centre mainly dates back to the early eighteenth century and boasts some wonderful features like Cheap Street with its quaint shops and a tiny stream bisecting the pavement. My late father who was determinedly pro-saic without knowing the meaning of the word, described the latter as an ideal solution to the being "caught short after a few pints at The Angel." Prostate problems can obviously become an obsession.

Unfortunately, Frome tends to be regarded in a similarly utilitarian fashion by many of its residents. The old shopping centre of Catherine Hill has fallen into disuse with locals reluctant to ascend its cobbled pavement. The boarded-up shop windows and "To Let" signs detract from Catherine Hill's gritty, historic charm. The hill is a spine from which one can detour down alleys and side streets built in the early days of the woollen industry when Frome was destined to be "The Manchester of the south".

Weavers cottages line the narrow streets. These pre-date the similar terraces of Victorian England. The rooms are tardis-deep and with cellars and roof space used to compensate for a lack of width, they suggest a more thoughtful method of housing the town's workforce than the later Liverpool-type houses of the Industrial Revolution. And yet Frome lacks a distinct vitality. It is hard to imagine a latter-day Lennon extolling the virtues of Willow Vale in the fashion of "Strawberry Fields" or Butts Hill giving birth to another "Penny Lane".

February 25ᵗʰ

At work I casually glance through the Glastonbury rag to discover the local nightclub is soon to host The Fab Beatles. The owner has been stringing me along for three months on the promise of a gig in March but has suddenly opted for an alternative who don't have the advantage of local support. Maybe they've undercut even our modest quotation. I want to write or phone to thank him for the wasted phone calls, publicity materials and offers of complimentary tickets but decide against. Instead I compose a letter as follows:

"Dear Sir,

I have heard that you are currently publicising a Beatles tribute night at Heroes Bar in March.

Not living in the Glastonbury area, I have little idea of what's going on and so am dependent on word of mouth. Am I to assume then, that our proposed evening is going ahead?

Please get in touch to confirm which Thursday you have in mind. At the moment we are available on all Thursdays in March, so no problems of availability should arise.

Will a get-in time of 6.30 p.m. be O.K?

We can provide the P.A. inclusive of cost if you prefer.

Please confirm in writing a.s.a.p.

With thanks... etc: etc:"

What a wag!

February 27th

I had imagined The Silent Whistle to be one of those elegant timber-beamed country pubs with brass light fittings and Victorian prints on the walls. In fact, like most pubs that look to rock bands to increase their trade, it is a somewhat dilapidated, careworn building of spurious historic value. The new tenants are making a concerted attempt to do the place up, starting with the toilets. This would account for the stripe of bottle green paint that now adorns my best leather jacket.

The back bar is a former skittle alley with a tiny stage at the far end. As a result, I spend the evening with a ride-cymbal neatly sandwiched between my buttocks. The changing room is once again a revealing "behind the scenes" insight into the licensing trade. Seven of us cram cheek by jowl into a freezing half-demolished storage outhouse amongst beer kegs, crockery, broken mirrors, instruments, bricks and spare rolls of flock wallpaper. The room is so cramped there is a fear that we may button ourselves together and go on linked like a chain gang. The broken mirrors are so stained and frosted up by cold breath that we have to apply one another's drawn-on moustaches with clumsy shivering hands. This gives the impression of having entered into a band-only backstage chocolate-eating competition. Mike tries to raise morale by suggesting that one day we'll have our own luxury dressing rooms.

"No, Mike," I reply, "this is as good as it gets. I'm afraid this is the nemesis of your career."

"Never mind," says Rob, "they say you play these kind of places once on the way up, and once on the way down."

"Yeah. He's booked us again next week," retorts Steve dryly, from behind a pile of disused optics.

The trench humour continues in a similar vein until someone violently breaks wind, bringing about a premature evacuation to the stage for an impressively punctual start to the show.

Actually, the bar is quite cosy and atmospheric. We are engaged on a "box-office" basis without guarantee but with all sales going to us. Anne has agreed to sell tickets on the door and we manage to attract about seventy customers. Whether the offer of Carlsberg Export at one pound fifty a pint increases our trade is a matter of conjecture. We end up with about ten pounds a man more than a usual pub gig and so the trip down to Dorset has been justified.

It's always inspiring to play before a packed audience even in a small space. There is a particular challenge involved in winning over a new audience that brings out the best in us. The usual gags about being the only Beatles tribute band actually older than the originals and giving up LSD for Viagra go down well. They join in the singing but are too tightly packed behind tables to dance. This gives added impetus to the songs with the greatest emotional range.

"Hey Jude" is one of the more obviously moving numbers

and is immediately followed in the second set by "With a Little Help From My Friends". Having presented the Ringo version following our "Sgt Pepper" opening, we stretch poetic licence and revive the number in the style of probably the greatest cover version of any Beatles song.

Now, I'm no Joe Cocker, but with the assistance of some cunning microphone technique, the retention of as much phlegm as I can muster and with the band really cutting loose, we turn out a powerful and stirringly soulful rendition. John, Mike and Steve even manage the girlie backing singers' voices with genuine conviction. On a night like tonight, it's enough to make the hairs stand up on the back of your wig.

Without pause for applause, we segue straight into "Get Back," the first in a string of dance numbers and the cue for the audience to get to their feet. "With a Little Help" seems to have them rooted in their seats, so I step down from the stage and grab the nearest female extrovert in the audience. As we start to jive, she catches her feet in my microphone cable which in turn tilts over the microphone stand onto two teenage boys in the front row and exports my pint of Carlsberg all over the stage.

The boys, reluctantly out for the night with their parents, appear even more acutely embarrassed by being drawn into the act. My dancing partner seems oblivious to the whole charade but her exhibitionism encourages everyone else to sit tight, afraid of being victims of association. "Get Back" indeed. My partner and I swing dangerously close to the room's solitary propane gas heater that is conveniently situated in front of the fire exit. When the song ends, John Freeman, never one to let a potentially humiliating experience pass, declares:

"I'll tell you what. It's a long time since he danced with a woman in front of a gas fire."

The Idiot's Guide... No: 2
With a Little Help From My Friends

Our drummer Stuart Berry (occassionally referred to as Taff)
does a great rendition of the second song on the *Pepper*
album. I often follow it with the well worn Lennonesque
joke: "It takes years of practice to sing that flat, you know."
This is hardly fair on Taff who is spot-on key but accurately
impersonates the distinctively blunt "Sing-a-long-a-Ringo"
style. The audience love joining in on the question and
answer phase: ("Would you believe in a love a first sight?"/
"Yes, I'm certain that it happens all the time"). The harmonies on backing vocals help give the song a style and texture
which would not be out of place in a stage musical. Quite
a number of Beatles songs draw on stage musical influences
such as "Honey Pie", "When I'm Sixty Four" and even "She
Loves You", (of which, more to follow).

The Joe Cocker version of "With a Little Help From My
Friends" turns the common time ballad into a blues-waltz
fusion with gospel backing vocals. The resigned but happy
Billy Shears is adapted by Cocker into an angst ridden, love-

sick old alchy who looks all set to crash on your floor after a hard night trying to smoke away his sorrows at your expense: "Mmm, I get high with a little help from my friends..."

The Cocker version also allows Rob Waller to wallow throughout in a good, sixties style Hammond organ riff without the burden of constantly keeping a hand free to flick from one keyboard sound to another.

"With a Little Help" is surely the best song Lennon and McCartney gave to Ringo. A pity then that Ringo's version has been eclipsed by Joe Cocker. The same could be said of "I Wanna be Your Man", half of which John and Paul knocked off in five minutes during a visit to a Rolling Stones rehearsal. Their gift to the Stones was a wise move. Richard's gritty guitar and Jagger's grinding vocal turned an average song into a raunchy R&B belter.

Although Ringo's vocal opportunities were fairly minimal in The Beatles, in covering their songs we have taken full advantage of his counterpart's ability to "cheat-in" extra harmonies that thicken out the sound and help compensate for studio reverb and double tracking. Oh, and Stuart also does the obligatory "Yellow Submarine" with more conviction than you might think it deserves.

March

March 2nd

Bastardising the Beatles has been more fulfilling than I could have imagined. If you can't succeed with originality, then copy the best. It sometimes occurs to me onstage, last Saturday being one of those occasions, what a humbling experience it is to revel in the borrowed glory of Lennon and McCartney's wonderful songs. I occasionally come over quite sentimental when I see what The Beatles clearly mean to those singing along with us. There is a real sense that we are engaging in a mutual fantasy. As much as we adopt the persona of the band, so they take on the character of a Beatles audience. The rhetoric of "All You Need Is Love" sometimes seems so sincere, even gurgled through a punter's pint glass, that I find I'm often choking the words through a lump in the throat the size of an ice cube.

The show always ends (before the usual carefully rehearsed encore) with the only song in the set not penned by Lennon, McCartney or Harrison: "Twist and Shout". I've read that they had to do it at the end of the recording session and in one take, because Lennon's voice was understandably knackered after shrieking frenetically through what must be the best party song ever. Despite fears of the voice being shot before the encore, I can rarely resist the temptation to belt out "Twist and Shout" like a man about to have his vocal chords removed. With the audience inevitably joining John and Mike in the responses to "shake it, shake it, shake it baby now" on the final verse, a shiver ascends from the base of my spine of sheer, hedonistic pleasure. If Lennon had not retired from the stage so early, he would never have needed all those "cathartic screaming sessions" to release his inner turmoil.

Moments like that help to account for the addiction that overwhelms the tribute artist. It is an addiction that often shakes me from marking essays, writing or watching a particularly gripping episode of *Coronation Street* to phone around for yet more bookings. With Les Battersby in low profile this evening, British Telecom shareholders are in for a bonus.

After ringing Terry at The Silent Whistle ostensibly to thank him for booking us on Saturday, I discover he is keen to do another gig in the summer, possibly outdoors. The dates we settle on coincide with Glastonbury. It would be nice to call it "The Glastonbury Alternative" in the hope of picking up custom from those whose VW Campers can't quite stagger all the way West to Worthy Farm.

Terry has kindly recommended us to The Central Hotel in Poole and I also persuade them to give us a gig in June. We are keen to make in-roads to the south coast scene and this venue would be a very credible start. He also makes tentative enquiries about Millennium New Year's Eve. Decisions need to be made.

March 4ᵗʰ

Thursday is Tony Stockley's day teaching drums at school. Tony and I first performed together before either of us knew of our Millfield connections. As a visiting peripatetic teacher, Tony has little contact with other members of staff, so we always make a point of meeting quietly for lunch so as to escape briefly into Dart Board Band gossip.

Tony is the only real full timer in the band, given that his entire working life is spent playing or teaching percussion.

Recently, his long-standing engagements in pit orchestras at places like the Theatre Royal Bath and Salisbury Playhouse have caused us to revert to our original drummer from the *All You Need is Love* show, Stuart "Taff" Berry. (Yes, racial stereotyping is alive and well in the West of England). Stuart was one of those who couldn't make the show's revival tour to Germany and the Czech Republic in '96, and thus lost out when commercial engagements followed. He was disappointed but was adaptable and understanding enough to stand in for Tony and by mutual agreement, is now back as our first call drummer.

Today I am desperate to commit Tony to a couple of dates in the summer when Taff is unavailable due to his wife Claudia expecting their first baby. I am also trying to persuade him to stand in for a possible Millennium New Year's Eve gig. Inevitably, Tony will be receiving other offers and can't afford the sentiment of taking a pay cut to play for us. I am under some pressure to commit the band to a booking in Hertfordshire on New Year's Eve for the biggest fee we may ever be offered but Stuart is not the only one with considerations of family.

I'm more than aware for the need of members to balance the band with family and day job commitments but I still find myself getting tetchy and authoritative when trying to organise gigs and being unable to get firm decisions on their individual availability. I'm reluctant to admit it's the teacher in me. John is much the same. When we once did a comedy routine under the pseudonym of "Les and Kev Miserables", Mike (then Theatre Director) booked us at the Merlin Theatre to support the comedian Simon Fanshawe. Within five minutes of meeting, Fanshawe had astutely worked out we were teachers. We were appalled, considering ourselves far too "street-wise" to be thus classified. Fanshawe then made a fuss about our warm-up act being too long, but was less choosy when later recycling one of our routines into his slot on BBC's *That's Life* programme.

Perhaps we "front men" are a necessary driving force but I have to remind myself that the more relaxed, easy going approach of Lester, Steve, Rob and Taff is the reason the band gain so much pleasure from the job. Wherever we are booked, for whatever fee, they do the gig with no complaints. Last year I booked us into the Olympiad Leisure Centre in Chippenham on a box office percentage. The apathy with which the centre publicised the show was best exemplified by the fact they chose to display a single poster, held up by one drawing pin on a board awash with out-of-date notices for the swimming club, on the back staircase leading to a private staff room. Only thirty people turned up (one of whom admitted that he had only heard about the show from a chance conversation at the vets), but the lads took their fifteen quid with equanimity. Somehow, stopping off after the show to pay our respects at the roadside where the great Eddie Cochrane was driven to his death, put it all into perspective. At our age, we're just happy to have families, jobs and still be playing rock'n'roll.

March 5th

A late night on theatre duty attending the school dance production. Brilliant show as usual undermined by the over-the-top, football crowd-type reaction from the pupils. On returning to lock the bar I find my briefcase has been stolen. No real valuables gone but the theatre diary is missing. This means possible chaos in re-booking all theatre events for the next four months. Worse still, a list of fifty potential venues and publicity letters for Sgt Pepper's Only Dart Board Band were in the case and are probably being thrown in the nearest river as I write.

March 11th

Paul Price phones re: Millennium gig. He wants a more definite commitment as to availability. Again, I have to stall. We have no drummer, Rob is having second thoughts about appearing on the big night and Mike has countered the idea by suggesting we throw our own big party. Performing gives me greater pleasure than partying and the last place I want to be on New Year's Eve is on a dance floor listening to another band entertaining for an obscenely lucrative fee that might otherwise have been ours.

Paul is my brother-in-law by marriage to Anne's sister, Cheryl. Paul organised the legendary event at Bishop's Stortford where, thanks to a disabled decibel limiter, we played one of our most enjoyable evenings. My mother arranged a coach party on the night for family and friends from Luton. Judging from my brother's drunken state on re-alighting, the vehicle is probably still being disinfected. The popularity of the event has spurned more sequels than *Star Trek*. Now Paul is helping organise a major celebration on New Year's Eve for residents of the elegant Hadham Hall estate where they live.

Hadham Hall is an Elizabethan Manor that became a boarding school. Since the closure of the school, the house was developed into swish apartments and has new houses built amongst the converted barns and stables in a style sympathetic enough to pacify most conservationists. The aim for December 31st is to plant a massive marquee on the central green and invite all two hundred residents plus extended families and friends.

Members of the residents' committee have been considering their options regarding the entertainment and another band has also been recommended. A deposition of eight residents was invited to attend a rehearsal last night for our rivals and so I am anxious to get Paul's response. Paul is not renowned for his subtlety:

"Crap," he barks down the phone. "They were bloody useless."

Getting Pricey on a topic on which he has firm opinions can make for an amusing Alf Garnett-like verbal diversion:

"Bloody embarrassing. Eight of us went. They were rehearsing in this office. I ask yer! You couldn't swing a cat! So we all sat there, like sardines, while they went through the act. 'Course, no one knew whether to clap. They finish a number, we'd all look at one another. Deathly bleedin' silence! I mean, I felt sorry for the bloke on the committee who recommended them. They couldn't play anything past 1967. 'Course we were all very tactful in the pub afterwards. You know, telling this geezer we'd got to keep our options open and all that. On the way back I made sure I wasn't in the same car. Just to get an honest opinion.

"Which was?"

"Unanimous. They stunk the place out."

I politely tell him that I wouldn't like to be judged myself on the basis of one rehearsal in an office. Of course, I'm quietly delighted and unknown to Pricey, punch the air as he lays into the opposition.

Laying into the opposition is something Paul was particularly good at during his career as a professional footballer. On one of the many phases in my earlier life when I was pathetically despairing of ever being some kind of success, Paul became part of the family and I was able to experience the next best thing. When Cheryl first met Paul he was the cool, unassuming captain of Luton Town in the old Second Division. Claiming Welsh nationality through his late father, Paul had begun to make an impression on the international scene with his debut in an historic 4-1 defeat of England at Wrexham. In the summer of 1981, Paul and Cheryl married and soon after, Paul achieved the dream transfer to the cup holders Tottenham Hotspur. At that time the Spurs team was one of the fondest in the fans' memory, featuring Ossie Ardiles, Ricky Villa and of course, Saint Glenn, Patron of the Lane. Despite serious injury in his first away game, Paul helped the team to the League Cup Final and a second successive FA Cup victory. My only regret was that all this happened when Anne and I were on the Isle of Wight and so we saw little of the action at close hand.

Having made that point, there were times when I discovered that being close to someone so renowned has its drawbacks. Paul's eminent years in football coincided with the exciting times spent with Ray Thomas building up the theatre programme and Drama Department at Medina High School. Visits by luminaries like Stephan Grappelli, Judy Dench and Rowan Atkinson coupled with the success of our own productions, had little effect on the folks back home. This was primarily because the Isle of Wight, though barely overseas, seemed distant and inaccessible. Worse still, whilst I was enjoying some of my long-term ambitions, my achievements on stages of the Isle of Wight were dwarfed by a brother-in-law whose theatre was White Hart Lane or Wembley Stadium.

Naturally I relished rather than resented Paul's success. After all it was not as if we were working in the same field. But on more than one occasion I began to consider whether or not I should have spent more seasons with the National Youth Theatre, gone to drama school rather than university and worked towards being a bit-part actor rather than a school teacher.

The despair did not last for long. I soon came to terms with reality and Paul's career went the way of all footballers, a salutary lesson in fame being a fickle mistress and all that.

In a draw in my study I keep a 1982 copy of the *Daily*

Being John Lennon

Mail. At the height of his fame, I managed to upstage Pricey. I had been cast as Frank Spencer in a stage adaptation of the television series *Some Mother's Do 'Ave 'Em!* The show was a "pilot" for a summer season run at the Prince Consort Theatre in Ryde. Local performers were chosen to try out the show during the Whitsun week. This led to a great deal of press interest resulting in a truly appalling picture of me in beret and raincoat, swinging through a window on an improbably placed chandelier, attempting to mouth the immortal words "Oooooh Betty" with no apologies to Michael Crawford. On the back page of the same paper, Paul also gets a mention in a Spurs match report.

Paul's promotion of the band at Bishop's Stortford was the first time many of our family and friends had seen me perform. My work in the theatre was either unknown or of no consequence to some of them. Many were genuinely surprised to see me in a Beatles tribute band and even more shocked that we were any good. It is the kind of "artistic" respect I tried so hard to achieve many years ago and had long ceased worrying about. In the last twenty years, much of my ego has been shed with my hair but there still lurks this sad desire for acknowledgement. That the catalyst for this belated recognition should be Paul Price may seem ironic. Not as ironic as the fact that, of the two of us, Pricey is the one who has achieved the rare distinction of appearing on *Top of the Pops*. ...Bloody football songs!

March 19th

First gig for three weeks. "The Underground" is a function bar in the cellar of The Rummer pub in Bristol. The show has been well publicised in the local press, and on regional TV in one of those appalling "let's take a look at the local rock scene" slots. Apparently our name gave rise to that phoney presenter-to-presenter jollity these local news programmes love to contrive. A poster on the street implores passers-by to "Come and see The Beatles down this Cavern". Only a Bristolian could construct in such a lexicological combination.

The place is in fact, wonderfully reminiscent of the Cavern with a low vaulted ceiling and tables made from wooden beer barrels. The stage entrance is via St. Nicholas Market, a glass-roofed Victorian building housing secondhand book and record stalls. Gas-style street lamps rise from disjointed pavements that echo with the footsteps of folk cutting through the market to the numerous surrounding pubs. The smell of the obligatory kebab kiosk and the muted throbbing of juke-boxes create the ambience of "a night out on the town." As we queue for a kebab pre-show (I play safe with a vegetable samosa), a group of local lads talk excitedly to their mates about how they're not "clubbing it tonight cause we're off to see the Beatles down the Rummer." Of course we resist the temptation to introduce ourselves.

The promoter, Joe, is celebrating his birthday and has invited a group of friends. This swells the audience to a respectable eighty-odd... not bad considering the competition in central Bristol. The "dressing room" is again the barrel store, but this one is no more than a cupboard. Mike immediately declares an embargo on the breaking of wind. This is rich coming from him.

In the long wait prior to performance, we sink a few pints in the bar upstairs. Hot on the gossip agenda is the precise identity of tonight's sound engineer, "Ellen" or possibly "Allen". On entering The Underground "Ellen" greets us from the opposite end of this lengthy cellar. At this point we are all curious to get a closer glimpse of this frail, husky-voiced siren with her waist-length blond tresses. On closer inspection "Ellen" appears distinctly flat-chested with traces of facial hair. Lester's "nice to meet you Allen" is met with an abrupt: "It's "Ayllen" actually" which is neither Ellen, Allen or enlightening. Freeman (somewhat typically) verifies the identification of a bra... but of negative cup-size. We are all none the wiser.

Conversation switches to fond reminiscences. The mention of the Glastonbury Festival is always synonymous with the word "toilets" and there follows a lengthy and amusing discourse on the more precise contents on the world's worst public conveniences, coupled with apocryphal stories of those who had actually fallen in the shit-pits and lived to tell the tale. Rob Waller, ever the master of the non-sequitur, manages to steer the conversation to the subject of concentration camps. To state that this is "a sensitive issue" earns no reward for intuition, but given that some of Rob's Polish relatives died in the camps makes one give even greater respect to the subject. Last year Rob went to Poland on a family visit but the serious intention of his anecdote is scuppered on the opening line:

"Last year, when we went to Auschwitz... on our summer holidays..."

Inevitable glances across the table.

At which point Lester in his slow, deliberate, mock-sincere West Country way replies:

"Tell me Rob. Was that half board... or self catering?"

Rob is unable to proceed with the story on account of the unashamed fit of hysteria that follows. Even Rob himself is reduced to watering his beer with tears of laughter. At least I hope they were from mirth.

The gig concludes in an orgy of drunken revelry and appreciation. Joe, the promoter, is delighted. Our cut of the revenue isn't great but we enjoy the night and are quick to accept the suggestion of a return booking. Joe recounts a story that turns into a back-handed compliment. Perhaps the greatest compliment we are ever likely to receive. Apparently two potential punters, descending the Underground steps, ask Joe what's on.

"It's a Beatles tribute night." He replies.

The punters stop for a moment, listen at the door and unexpectedly put their wallets away.

"You must be joking mate," says one. "I'm not paying for that. That's a bloody tape!"

March 20th

Six forty-five a.m.. The alarm sounds. It's Saturday morning. I have to work. I have had four hours sleep. I am dehydrated. Three pints of Worthington seem to have been directly transfused into my blood stream. I now wish I had doubled my intake simply to make this hangover worthwhile. I do not smoke, but last night inhaled enough nicotine whilst singing to tarmac the M5. I then remember I have to referee the third eleven this afternoon and so reach for the Paracetemol.

March 22nd

Rob, Stuart and Mike all declare themselves out for Millennium New Year's Eve. Lester looks unlikely. John, Steve and I will have to cobble a line up together for the Bishop's Stortford do. The promoters want us to play a wide variety of material other than Beatles so we will have to rehearse extensively. I phone Steve Hurd to tell him.

Steve interrupts my flow almost immediately. "Er, can we go for a pint? Only we need to talk." Alarm bells start to ring as I head for The Farmer's Arms, just two hundred yards down the road. Steve is already there, half-way through his first pint of Usher's Best. We sit down. Steve is never one to equivocate. "I've decided to leave the band," he informs me.

Steve is a tall imposing figure onstage. His bass playing is solid yet deft. In the Sgt Pepper team, Steve is the centre half. He's like a Tony Adams of a few years ago, only without the drink problem. Steve is the central mast of the circus tent around which the rest of us attempt to drape, elegantly. His decision is completely unexpected.

Steve recently stood-in for another local band The Skooters. It turns out that they've asked him to become a permanent member. Steve suggests that he needs a new challenge after four years of Beatles music. This I can appreciate, but when we go through diaries to work out a retirement date, I note that The Skooters (or is it "Skaters?") are limited to the kind of pub gigs we play only when nothing better comes along. I suspect family reasons have influenced Steve's decision.

The worst of all this is The Skeemers are a re-formation of John's old band The Havana Fireflies. John was the bassist, vocalist and leading songwriter with the Fireflies for ten years. In that time they privately released two impressive albums, performed on TV soundtracks and earned an excellent reputation on the West Country circuit. Gradually the group diversified into separate projects including The Skoders, who began cashing in on the success of the Fireflies — minus John. Steve's defection has not helped ease the animosity that sprang from the Fireflies acrimonious split.

Once he has given me the bad news, Steve steers the conversation round to reminiscing about all the shows we had worked on over the last eleven years. It is an impressive list: *Godspell, Tommy, The Wall, Defectors* (one of my many attempts at a hit musical), *All You Need is Love* and *Waterloo Sunset* amongst them. We have played before audiences as small as two and (on Bath Festival opening night in '93) as large as twenty thousand. We have taken shows to Germany and the Czech Republic. We have shared the unique experience of appearing in tribute bands to The Who and The Beatles. It feels as if Steve is signing off for good.

I get back home and ring John. His reaction is muted,

appearing almost unsurprised. We turn our attentions to a replacement.

"What about you?" I suggest.

"I'll think about it," he replies.

March 23rd

I sleep badly, worrying about the implications of Steve's imminent departure. The post arrives, including a letter from the Cheese and Grain Hall. Anticipating this to be a bill or some attempt to waive our fee, I reluctantly split the envelope. A cheque is enclosed. It is seventy five pounds more than I was expecting for our performance six weeks ago. I am bemused. Reading to the bottom of the page, I discover that this time they are victims of their own inefficiency. Having failed to properly arrange contracts, the management have assumed us to be on a 70% cut of profit as we had been in October. In fact, we agreed to reduce our percentage to 50%. I wake the kids by laughing like a drain.

John calls early evening. He's thought about it. He'd like to play bass. Stuart Berry and I drive over to John's to discuss things further. Stuart as the drummer, is most affected by Steve's departure. They have developed a superb on-stage relationship and Taff's drumming exudes a confidence now that owes a lot to Steve's dependable rhythm.

I suspect John is galvanised by the determination to thwart The Skooters evil plan of local domination. He faces the difficulty of learning a two-hour set, as well as having to concentrate on singing, making gags and keeping up the "Paul Lemmon" personality. Having three of the Beatles up front as vocalists makes Sgt Pepper's Only Dart Board Band unique and, in its own peculiar way, very effective. We always explain our reluctance to play our own instruments on stage as down to arthritis and the fact that we were no good anyway. Audiences never seem perturbed by this. With John playing bass it may be necessary for me to pick up a guitar to complete the picture. Fortunately, there is no need for me to be heard. Mike has a bigger problem in that he doesn't play drums and needs to be in the front line. We conceive the idea of Mike doing assorted percussion and sound effects. His dog impression on "Hey Bulldog" is (I'm rather reluctant to admit) a highlight on which we might build. We envisage a prop table with the fireman's bell from "Penny Lane" and the alarm clock from "A Day in the Life" amongst other effects. These should be played with the precise presentation technique of a Victorian music hall magician. Mike, as a former actor (once of *Coronation Street* no less), does this kind of thing with great panache.

Afterwards we try playing a few of the easier songs with John busking on the bass. A big advantage of John playing bass is financial, in that we will become a more compact six piece unit. Optimism prevails.

March 24th

Olivia's eleventh birthday. Last Sunday she passed her grade one drum exam with honours, much thanks to Tony Stockley's expert teaching. I am delighted, but resolve that my family will not become the new Osmonds.

March 25th

Back to The Riverside, Bradford on Avon. Peter, the landlord has tabled a provisional offer for Millennium New Year's Eve and is disappointed we're not available. I suspect the fee would have come down on his original offer anyway, especially as he short-changed us by twenty five quid on the night's cut. With Steve leaving in May and no guarantee of Lester's involvement, Sgt Pepper will be going out on New Year's Eve as a duo. I had hoped Steve's son Alex may step in but that is now less than plausible. Anne is pushing hard for the solution of Tom, Richard and Olivia on guitar, bass and drums for the occasion. I am about to ask her if she would also like us to play some Osmonds' numbers, then I remember her record collection from the early seventies and refuse to tempt providence.

March 26th

Richard's fourteenth birthday. With Thomas about to turn sixteen next week, March is like Christmas again as far as the Dimery bank account is concerned. Don't ask me why they were all born in March. And no, conception does not coincide with our wedding anniversary, either of our birthdays or observation of the outbreak of World War Two.

For his birthday, Rich has acquired a rather nice second-hand electric guitar complete with Floyd Rose string locks. These, my wife refers to as "those Lloyd-George things."

School finishes for Easter. And not a day too soon.

A long Parents Consultation afternoon ends with me the last to leave and hurriedly debriefing Chris Jagger on the follies of Jagger Minor on my way to the car.

"So, getting many gigs, Mart?" he drawls.

"Not bad, Chris. You see, we're all local. We can afford to take small fees if we're not travelling too far. Obviously, your lads need a good guarantee before they'll trek out from London."

"Yeah right. Still, I could join your band. I could do John Lennon," he observes.

"Now that would be a novelty," I reply.

March 27th

Swish wedding at a posh hotel in Sherborne, Dorset. Weddings are a cinch. Captive audience and everybody's drunk. The bride, Siobhan, I know from work. The groom Steve, is a helicopter pilot in the Navy. The place is full of uniforms, so "Lovely Rita" we dedicate "to all the traffic wardens here tonight."

In the last week there have been NATO strikes on Serbia

following the Kosovo crisis. A few years ago, this kind of thing used to worry me. In fact, I probably would have turned it into an angst-ridden stage musical. Now I'm learning to write about matters other than major wars and revolution. Maybe I'm just getting into middle-aged complacency. Anyway, thankfully for the happy couple, the groom's avoided the call to arms so far and they should get the honeymoon in before further developments. "All You Need is Love" goes down particularly well.

March 31st

Thomas's sixteenth birthday. My sweet little boy now towers over me and seems to be going through a rapid fast-forward of the biological clock. His first "official" girlfriend, Willow, is dominating his social life and suddenly Anne and I have become peripheral figures in his future. He stays out late, goes to parties and is doing most of the things expected of teenagers. I lay awake worrying where he's got to. I knew this day would arrive, but it doesn't make it any easier.

Yesterday an old friend and colleague from the Isle of Wight, Bernie Gilman, paid us a visit. We haven't met in fifteen years and Bernie takes great delight in finding me the balder of us both. Bernie's first wife Claire, presented us with a beautiful book of photographs when Tom was born and these have inevitably been aired again on his birthday.

Anne and I were very close to Bernie and Claire but like Bernie, we have completely lost touch with the latter. Bernie is one of the funniest people I know. We appeared in many sketches together at the Medina Theatre and he even drummed in the first musical show I wrote entitled *Graven Image*. Our contact in the intervening years has been scant but yesterday it is as if we'd never been apart. Bernie's life has followed an extraordinary pattern.

Obviously my influence on Bernie was less than constructive. Almost immediately following my departure from

Medina High School he was rapidly promoted to Deputy Headmaster. An Inspector's job in Derbyshire followed, before they were all laid off thanks to Thatcherite privatisation. Bernie then went back to his original stomping ground of Essex to become a Headmaster.

Having turned round a failing school, he looked proudly out of his study window one day across the school playing field to see two men in suits stalking the property. Bernie accosted them. They were quantity surveyors. The County Council had failed to inform Bernie that his school was about to be closed and the land sold off to Ford of Dagenham. Despite the suggestion of Bernie retaining his headship after amalgamation to a neighbouring school, he took the moral high ground all the way to Lowestoft. Bernie gives good political reasons for his brief tenure as a headmaster in Lowestoft but I cannot help but think that his current partner, Karina, had a part to play in matters. Karina is a delightful dentist from Denmark and fourteen years Bernie's junior. They now live in Copenhagen. Bernie has been doing odd jobs like delivering papers but they will soon be departing for an International School in Kuwait where he will return to classroom teaching. It is a sign of the pressures in state education when a talented, experienced professional like Bernie can just give it all up... albeit at the snap of a dishy Danish dentist's surgical glove.

I write this in the dead of night unable to sleep, as eight of Tom's friends, having gathered here to honour his birthday, wander in and out of the house to smoke cigarettes and skateboard down our drive. Korn and Green Day blast from the downstairs stereo. The former sounds to me like the yelping and barking of a frightened dog trapped in the boot of a crashed car. Oh God! I'm turning into my parents!

Being John Lennon

The Idiot's Guide... No: 3
Twist and Shout

"Leather Lungs Lennon" was an early epithet for The Beatles most high profile member. The name was an accurate description to anyone fortunate to have heard the Fab Four live. I actually did hear The Beatles once. I must have been seven or eight at the time. My father needed to drive into Luton town centre one evening to post a letter. It was probably some kind of Rates demand which he had neurotically filled in on the instant of arrival and was desperate to dispatch. Poor old Tony, never got much peace of mind in this life. We parked outside the old Ritz Cinema where a small gaggle of teenage girls had gathered and were squealing and jumping to the sounds within. "Hey! Come and listen to this" said dad, taking my hand and leading me from the car. I put my ear up to the carefully guarded doors of the Ritz and from inside came the unmistakable grainy, powerful and sexually charged cravings of Lennon telling us all about his "Hard Day's Night".

"Twist and Shout" was just one of the early cover versions

of rock'n'roll classics to which Lennon was able to bring that distinctive and plaintive raw edge. "Money", "Dizzy Miss Lizzy" and "Bad Boy" all suited his earthy range. John Lennon did for "Twist and Shout" what Cocker did for "With a Little Help From My Friends". It is often forgotten that "Twist and Shout" is a Medley-Russell composition, not Lennon-McCartney. Indeed, to illustrate the point, I have completely forgotten the original recording artist and can't be arsed to find out. It is of course an Americanised reworking of "La Bamba" which further clouds the issue. Infact, with the addition of Rob's keyboard, the Dart Board Band's version drifts a little towards the Latin feel. The song always ends the set because it is impossible not to dance to. We've witnessed punters standing on tables and chairs to find the room to swing their sometimes considerable hips.

The song best illustrates the raw energy of the early Beatles, suggesting why they were a popular live act in Liverpool and Hamburg. The drift into experimental sounds and ballads at the expense of the rock'n'roll hits came when they had retired from live performance but as "Get Back" and "One After 909" suggest, they were to return to their rock roots during the final *Let it Be* phase.

John Freeman and I originally shared vocals in the seminal "All You Need is Love" show according to personal preference and range, rather than which Beatle we were impersonating. This has continued to be the case to some extent. John is by far the better harmony singer. He can lock on to a line and hold it with little wavering from the first rehearsal. It takes me hours to learn harmonies. On the other hand, I probably have a wider range and so it better suits my voice to do the McCartney ballads like "She's Leaving Home", "Yesterday" and "Hey Jude". John, though does a cracking job on "A Hard Day's Night", "Revolution" and "I Feel Fine" which is just as well, as neither of us could easily sustain that gravelly Lennon sound for two and a half hours a night. I don't know how the bloody hell he managed. Must have been all that chain smoking and the Mersey air.

April

April 10th

Arrive at the sprawling hell-hole otherwise known as London Gatwick Airport, having smuggled Tom through customs after belatedly realising he had just passed the age requiring an adult passport. Glad to be back after an indifferent holiday in France.

The pleasure soon wore thin on stepping over the familiar threshold. My situation comedy script has been rejected by the BBC, I have no news regarding the teaching job I applied for two weeks ago and the answerphone contains the following message:

(High squeaky but earnest voice): "Hallo, David here, Phoenix Arts Centre, Hastings. About your gig next Saturday. I think it might be a good idea to cancel. We've only sold two tickets. Trouble is, they've got a Stones tribute on at Bexhill the same night."

Bearing in mind that the two tickets were probably friends invited by Steve and that we were on 70% of the box office, I decide that a second trip around the southbound M25 in seven days might be better avoided. What is it about Stones tribute bands?

April 14th

Dust off my old Hofner Verithin semi-acoustic guitar. It's a bit of a collectors' item dating back to about 1960 and probably worth a few bob back then. Nowadays you can get a better sounding Japanese Stratocaster copy for not much more than a hundred pounds. The Hofner is now valued at nearer five hundred. My brother Paul, a used car dealer with an eye for a bargain, picked it up for eighty quid about twelve years ago.

I intend to use the guitar in our re-vamped line-up, not so much for the sound as its authentic look. In truth, the modern cheap, Tanglewood copy of the John Lennon Rickenbacker would probably sound a lot better. The Tanglewood company is owned by the father of a pupil. They've offered me a copy at a handsome discount, probably the equivalent of a year's wages for some waif-like worker slaving in their Korean sweat-shop. The post-holiday economic recession (rather than the principle of exploiting the third world), makes me decide to renovate the Hofner which has the advantage of being both genuine and quite similar to George Harrison's Gretsch guitar. My friend at a local Music Workshop tells me there's not much wrong with it that can't be cured by replacing "what appear to be the original strings."

I'm learning about twenty of our thirty-five song set. The rest will be best left uncorrupted. The magnitude of John's task in learning bass parts for the whole programme is only just beginning to sink in.

On my way to the Music Workshop I cannot resist calling in at The Memorial Hall who are advertising "the best tribute band in the world". This happens to be (in case you were unaware) *The Anthology of The Beatles Show*, featuring two look-a-likes Gary Gibson and Lawrence Gilmour. Interestingly, their backing band, like ourselves, stretches the line-up to substantially more than a fab four.

As we are playing on Friday, we'll miss the opportunity to check out the opposition. This lot have played some major theatres and Gibson has raised his Lennon-like profile in a recent British Telecom commercial with "TV personality"

Chris (I'm not an over-paid megalomaniac) Evans. Gilmour appeared as McCartney on *Stars in Their Eyes,* a TV talent show whose sole purpose is to discover people who are incapable of originality.

The trouble with being eerily like one's role model is that the show must surely become over-reverential. When one has got over the initial shock of how much they look like the real thing, what greater surprises are then held in store?

Anyway, if this is just sounding like sour grapes, I can only say that when I heard from the box office manager that the show was struggling to raise a modest audience, I greeted the fact with the all gravity and sensitivity the matter warranted, until a safe distance from the building, that is. Woo hoo!

April 15ᵗʰ - I read the news today...

A Millfield girl has been murdered. Ashleigh Robinson's body was found in an alley in Guildford. She had been strangled.

I didn't know the girl. But as soon as the news broke, identifying the victim only as a Somerset girl, I guessed she was from Millfield. Many pupils live in the Surrey stockbroker belt and it turns out Ashleigh had travelled from her Axbridge home to attend a joint birthday celebration for three students. There were many other Millfieldians present. Ashleigh left the club accompanied by a twenty-nine year old man. He has been arrested.

Last summer term, whilst also celebrating her birthday, a fourteen year old pupil fell from the roof of her boarding house. She died shortly afterwards. During the summer holidays two pupils who had recently left the school were killed in accidents. One died in the Swissair disaster in Canada, the other lost control of his new motorbike. The bike was a present... for the boy's birthday.

Past controversies have been stirred up by the press in

reporting these and other tragic or incidents this year. Always they mention "the fifteen thousand pounds a year" fees, the exotic amenities and celebrity pupils of the past. Usually they manage to mention Ian Botham, confusing Millfield with Millford in Yeovil. The impression given of Millfield is that of a liberal "Club 18-30" holiday environment where cosseted offspring of the rich become drunk and take drugs with alarming frequency. The *Daily Mail*, in particular, seems to have the knack of unearthing every disillusioned pupil to have passed through the portals of the school at any time in the last sixty years and gives them a platform for their shallow grievances.

This terrible murder has been given considerable column space in this morning's papers focusing on Ashleigh's associations with "one of the country's top public schools." The fact she was beautiful, talented, intelligent and from a wealthy background is paraded before us. At what point, I wonder, will the press begin to connect this horrifying tragedy with superfluous intimations of the decadent lifestyle our pupils are supposed to lead?

The grief we must face on returning to school after Easter has become all too familiar. This single, brutal, violent, death will overwhelm many students. It will be impossible to reconcile their own futures and the impending A-Level exams with the futility and emptiness this act of savagery has caused.

Meanwhile on T.V. and in the newspapers, a convoy of Kosovo refugees; over sixty men, women and children, obliterated by the fire of misguided NATO missiles, is being casually referred to as "collateral damage."

April 16th

Alan Fordham is a neighbour of the Price's. Now, as attractive as it is, the executive housing development at Hadham Hall is hardly millionaire's row. When Alan offered to book

Sgt Pepper at the Golf Club he owns, I had assumed from his own property, that the business would incorporate a pleasant, but relatively modest clubhouse. As I approach the club, scene of tonight's performance, I realise I could not have been more mistaken. Hertfordshire Golf Club is a massive Victorian mansion, close to the fleshpots of Broxbourne and Cheshunt. There was more money manifest in the car park than even Millfield on Parents Day.

We have been booked as an after-dinner act in the club restaurant. I took the booking with the intention of staying overnight before making our way south to Hastings. With Hastings now postponed, my wisdom in dragging the band all the way up the M25 in the Friday night rush-hour is subject to question. Furthermore, I'd reduced the fee in return for accommodation which is now unnecessary.

Worries are eased as the band eventually join the advanced party of Steve, Lester and I after navigating the M25 madness. The restaurant is full but the elegant decor engenders a polite ambience and the audience is clearly going to take a bit of warming up. After the usual opening of "Sgt Pepper's Lonely Hearts Club Band" we segue into a Ringo-style "With A Little Help From My Friends". Lester's guitar solo linking the two songs unexpectedly sounds like the subsequent wail of a scabby tom-cat when struck on the arse by an air gun pellet. I look around to see that Lester is incapacitated by a broken string. The band stumbles to a grinding halt but I quickly count us all back in and Rob carries the melody on keyboard whilst Lester dashes off to change the string. Quick as a flash, I see my chance to put into operation some of the guitar parts I've been practising. I grab Rob's spare guitar he uses for occasionally filling-in and begin playing along. Unfortunately, I can barely remember a single chord, and before long find myself turning down and miming in the desperate hope nobody in the audience actually realises.

Lester's return is a welcome relief and by the end of the first set we are on good form. Not realising there was another hour to come, a punter catches us in the interval, thinking we are about to leave and promptly books us to play a wedding at Hanbury Manor, another posh country club further up the A10.

"It's a real pukka place. It's where Gazza and Sheryl got spliced," he proudly boasts.

"An ominous start to the marriage then," I retort, but the irony is lost.

As our rooms are still available in the club, John and I decide to defer the long drive back until the morning; a decision which has absolutely nothing to do with the club's preponderance of pretty French waitresses, no matter what Mike Walker thinks.

April 16th

Eating breakfast on a dazzling Saturday morning overlooking the first tee, John and I reflect on the possibilities of targeting more golf and country clubs. It seems that bookings are gathering momentum and fees beginning to reflect the hours of labour each gig brings. We wonder how Steve feels listening to the rest of us chewing over offers and whether he has any regrets about leaving.

By the time I get home, the happy couple has already left a message, desperate to acquire our services for their nuptials at Hanbury Manor. The 29th May is free and so another circumnavigation of the M25 beckons.

April 22nd

Teenagers are amazingly resilient. Despite the horror of the recent murder, most at Millfield already seem to be back into the usual routine. This week's massacre of schoolchildren by two of their number in Colorado and the continuing atrocities in Yugoslavia are perhaps numbing the students' sense of tragedy.

A good day all round. Tony Stockley confirms that he will cover for Stuart on Millennium New Year's Eve. *The Stage* newspaper is to publish an extract from this diary in next week's "Tribute Band Supplement" (surely a "must" for all serious music lovers); and I am to be granted an interview for the post of Head of Drama at Prior Park College in Bath, next Thursday.

April 25th

Return home following weekend double-header. After being offered a Sunday lunchtime booking at the Officer's Mess at an RAF Station near Shrewsbury, I spend many hours on the phone pleading for a Saturday night gig en-route, so as to break up the journey. Finally, I concede to a ridiculously low offer from Wolverhampton University which will just about pay our expenses for the trip.

The Student Union bar is a massive 'L' shaped room with a dance floor and stage at one end. We are somewhat apprehensive at playing to a student audience, assuming they might give us a cynical response. Actually they are very quiet and it is not until well into the second half that the bar fills and an atmosphere slightly warmer than Greenland develops. All too late in the evening the studiously cool are seriously drunk and the dance floor fills with weak-kneed scholars celebrating another extension to their student overdraft.

The gig also provides another worthy of entry into the *Rough Guide to Dressing Rooms*. Actually, the rooms are quite comfortable offices, but situated along such a labyrinth of corridors and stairs that they prove near impossible to find during the interval. Desperate for a leak prior to the second half and not wishing to put in an appearance fully costumed in the nearest public lavatory, Mike, John and I sneak through the emergency exit backstage and relieve ourselves behind a corporation skip. Not unusually, our timing is out and we find ourselves listening to the introduction of "I Am the Walrus" mid-stream. Risking the residue of "yellow matter custard" down the front of my frock-coat I dash for the stage just in time to begin the song. Mike, who clearly has the bladder retention of a moderately large camel, was still slashing up against the skip half-way through the first chorus, arriving just in time for "boy you've been a naughty girl, you let your knickers down".

We stay overnight with John's partner Louise, in Birmingham. John navigates our fleet of cars half-way to Coventry before we finally arrive in Acock's Green courtesy of a decidedly illegal manoeuvre on the M42. Lou's large terraced house is ideal for the band but for reasons of hygiene, I find myself less than inclined to share a double-bed with any of my sweaty comrades and so spend a restless night on the sofa.

After breakfast, Lou escorts us all to the front door with a gentle kiss on the cheek, except of course for John, who is entitled more than most to something resembling a parting snog. All of which causes great curiosity to the elderly West Indian gentleman in the house opposite who is making the most of sweeping the pavement as he counts seven men leaving the house. The quizzical look on his face is easy to interpret: "What is it coming to when a respectable area such as dis am gettin' houses of ill-repute?"

RAF Shorbury Officers' Mess could not be a greater contrast to Wolverhampton Uni. The entire place resembled the set of a post-war Ealing Comedy. Portraits of the Queen looking like a young Elizabeth Taylor adorn the walls. The whole building positively gleams. They probably spent the equivalent of the Shropshire road maintenance budget on

Brasso alone. There was even a Morris Minor in the car park.

The booking is courtesy of a very amiable Flight Lieutenant who had seen us perform the previous summer on his family holiday at The Millfield Holiday Village. Though we queried why anyone trapped in an institution all year round should want to spend his holidays at a public school, he was anything but the stereotypical RAF type. Unfortunately, his enthusiasm for our act had not spread to the younger trainee pilots on the base and our audience consisted of about five mature couples their children and their children's friends. All were seated in deep, comfortable armchairs in a room that had all the ambience of a doctor's surgery. It was like playing in an over-funded orphanage.

Let it be said however, that the Dart Board Band is not one to pass a gift-horse through the eye of a needle. We gratefully took the money, ate the complimentary lunch and did our best to make our friend the Flight Lieutenant believe we'd had the time of our lives.

April 26th

Kosovo; Denver; nail bombs in Brixton and Brick Lane and the death of Ashleigh Robinson have brought tragedy and savagery close to our thoughts. The untimely death of a celebrity though, brings out a different kind of despair. The deaths of Kennedy, Elvis and John Lennon were benchmarks in people's lives. The death of Princess Diana brought the public onto the streets in an unprecedented outpouring of grief. Despite these icons manifest weaknesses as human beings, many people somehow thought they knew and could identify with them. They were mourned as one mourns the loss of innocence and youth.

Jill Dando, as a celebrity, was by no means in that exalted league, which in some ways makes her murder today all the more poignant and closer to home. Never once did Jill

Dando use her celebrity to tell people how they should live their lives. The nearest she came was advising them how to spend their summer holidays or, on BBC's *Crimewatch* programme, warning them to look out for mysterious figures who could "be dangerous if challenged." Lennon and Diana flirted with controversy, manipulated the media to their own ends and made enemies as well as friends. Jill Dando never stopped being a down-to-earth Weston-Super-Mare girl who one could imagine being happy and fulfilled as a housewife or teacher or doctor. She just happened to choose journalism. Her career was a natural, steady progression: Local newspaper; local radio; regional television; breakfast newscaster; prime-time newscaster and finally, magazine-show host. Only last week, when she appeared posing before the bonnet of an Aston Martin on the cover of the *Radio Times*, sporting an outfit in Emma Peel leather, did I feel she might have become a victim of her own fame. TV executives and producers have a great deal to answer for when playing up the sex appeal of the likes of Jill Dando and Carol Vordermann. The whole point of their charm is their ordinariness. They are attractive but approachable "girls next door" who might be imagined, but never seen publicly, in anything more erotic than a twin set and pearls.

I remember well my one and only encounter with Jill Dando. It was the day of the 1990 World Cup Final. England should have been there of course, but thanks to the limitless luck of the Germans, we were to spend the afternoon basking in a glorious welcome in that hot-bed of so many British heroes, Luton.

I had once again been busy trying to negotiate a radio recording of *A Beatle Remembers,* my monologue on the life of John Lennon. Whilst trying to interest Vicki Klein, a radio producer at BBC Bristol in the project, she suggested I might like to appear on a Sunday morning radio show as a guest on the "Ardent Fans" slot. This feature was an opportunity for some of the West's saddest obsessives to gain public airtime when psychiatric help would have probably been more beneficial. Jill Dando was the highly tolerant host of the show. Despite her growing reputation as a national TV broadcaster, Jill still found time to drive "home" on a Sunday morning for this innocuous, incidental little programme.

I arrived in the studio as Jill played my introductory link, "Imagine". She had not been briefed as to my reason for being on the show and in the ensuing two minutes, I rapidly told her the questions to ask. I had become something of an old hand at conducting media interviews about the Lennon connection and she seemed grateful to have me holding the harness whilst she flew through the broadcast by "the seat of her pants". We soon relaxed into a lengthy interview in which I did everything possible to impress that I was a writer rather than some kind of Beatlemaniac. In the breaks whilst records were played, we chatted a little about Jill's brother Nigel, who, for his sins, was the *Bristol Evening Post*'s correspondent in Frome – a challenging post for the creative reporter, if ever there was one. Nigel had given *A Beatle Remembers* a glowing review in the *Post* and possessed many of the same virtues as his sister in a profession not renowned for its sincerity.

Jill was indeed utterly charming in an unforced, easy manner. If ever, God forbid, I find myself recuperating in the ward of National Health hospital, nothing could lift my spirits so readily as to be nursed through my recovery by the medical equivalent to Jill Dando. An elderly friend, being the type for whom these broadcasts seem to depend for an audience, remarked on the "sexual chemistry" evoked by our conversation. As the only experiments in chemistry I ever performed successfully resulted in the emission of insidious toxic gases, I wondered exactly what she meant.

Had England reached the World Cup Final that day, I like to think that I would have surprised the listeners by making an unanticipated and tearful recital of the Agincourt speech from *Henry V*. This, of course, would have so impressed Jill that she would have immediately invited me to make a repeat performance on the *Breakfast News* the next morning. Mercifully, a penalty shoot-out in Turin spared us both the embarrassment. The interview ended with me confirming that I would never lower myself to appearing in a wig on the cabaret circuit. I've always been full of shit, I suppose.

Jill Dando was unchanged by her achievements. She was one celebrity of whom no one could begrudge success. In the years since our brief encounter, I've watched her career flourish and taken pleasure in the thought that sometimes the good really do come out on top. It seems unfathomable that while we contemplated the murder of John Lennon on that bright summer Sunday in 1990, that some 10 years later Jill would also die on her doorstep at the hands of a gunman.

April 29th

Interview day. Prior Park College sits high on Claverton Down. The mansion house that now incorporates incomparably elegant classrooms and offices, looks down upon a Capability Brown landscape and beyond to the Georgian terraces and crescents of Bath Spa.

Less than twenty minutes along the glorious winding roads from Frome, Prior Park's obvious charms needed rationalising carefully before I could commit myself to returning to teaching Drama. My initial reservations were soon dispelled. The school's Julian Slade Theatre built for them by ex-pupil Sir Cameron Macintosh, was disappointingly under-equipped and a little cramped, but the staff appeared happy and the kids seemed reassuringly normal. I was required to teach a lesson under observation which I felt went well despite having never taught eleven-year-olds. Four years of ring-rust soon wore off, but I was secretly pleased to learn afterwards that the lucky applicant would be too tied up with sixth form teaching to spend much time with these irrepressibly excitable youngsters.

In short, I had become firmly re-acquainted with the familiar smell of greasepaint and sweaty plimsolls and was ready to encounter again the annual shock to the nervous system commonly known as the school play.

7.10 p.m.

Perhaps a simple letter of rejection would have been kinder. I learn tonight that I am not to be offered the appointment. The Headmaster seems unwilling to dwell on the telephone, so I shall never know why. It would have been preferable to have been given some reason, instead I spend the rest of the evening contemplating whether I was considered too old; too out of touch; too arrogant; too expensive (ha ha); or simply not up to it. Or maybe Sir Cameron phoned the Head warning him that *The Stage* this morning featured a compromising full colour photograph of one of the candidates wearing a ridiculous wig and purporting to be some kind of tribute band performer. A fact I conveniently failed to mention on my CV.

One consolation however: One or two colleagues at Millfield may be even more devastated that I'm staying than me.

The Idiot's Guide... No: 4
I Am The Walrus

In many ways the above song has shaped the approach and style of Sgt Pepper's Only Dart Board Band as a Beatles tribute. It featured prominently in the 1995 production of *All You Need is Love* at the ECOS Amphitheatre in Frome. "I Am The Walrus" was reprised throughout as a menacing theme for the Blue Meanies as previously seen in the film *Yellow Submarine*. It was clear from the outset that a good keyboard player would need to be on board our particular vessel if songs from the *Magical Mystery Tour* and *Sgt Pepper's Lonely Hearts Club Band* albums were not to leak and sink. Originally Simon Horsey, with whom I had composed a couple of stage musicals, took on the job. Simon is a superb, instinctive musician and we were very concerned when he became unavailable for the revival of the show in Germany and the Czech Republic which, in turn, led to the spin-off tribute band. Fortunately, Rob Waller stepped on board and with single minded determination plugged all the holes, even dismissing the use of click tracks for more complex pieces.

"I Am The Walrus" is a nonsense song in the style of "Jabberwocky" by Lewis Carroll. It's easy to suggest that drugs were the main inspiration for Lennon's absurd lyric. Infact, he had long been influenced by Carroll and the the humour of The Goons. His own verse and cartoons featured in the books *In Me Own Write* and *A Spaniard in the Works* bear great similarities to the work of Spike Milligan.

While we're on the subject of The Goons, am I the only one to have noticed a clear physical resemblance between Lennon and Goon actor Peter Sellers? Furthermore, the *Monty Python* team have often referred to The Goons as one of their great influences and yet look again at the films *A Hard Day's Night* and *Help* and notice how the twisted logic of the dialogue and plotlines make The Beatles a clear link between the absurd verbal radio humour of The Goons and its visual counterpart *Python*. Even *Yellow Submarine* can be seen as a forerunner of Terry Gilliam's anarchic cartoons in *Monty Python's Flying Circus* which surely owes its title to the Beatles popularisation of quirky Victoriana. Infact, now I think about it, John Lennon was probably the secret love child of Peter Sellers himself. (Sellers would have been 14 at the time of conception but why let facts stand in the way of a brilliant and revealing tabloid scandal?)

"Walrus" has probably been a trademark number for the Dart Board Band. With the orchestrations only slightly simplified by Rob and the words spread between John and myself like a musical dialogue, the song has great onstage energy perhaps because we tend to play it a little up tempo compared to the record. I suspect few other Beatles tributes would be able to get as close to the original and make it swing in quite the same way. During the fade out talk-overs, John and I can be faintly heard quoting famous lines from the Marx Brothers such as: "Marry me darling and I promise I'll never look at another horse again!" and "I can see you standing by the stove. I can see you but I can't see the stove." Now Groucho and co were a great influence on The Goons who... oh never mind, the connections become ever more tenuous and tedious.

May

May 1st

The last time Anne and I attended a function at the Silsoe Agricultural College it was to celebrate the Golden Wedding Anniversary of our old school play director, Derek Horsler. A few years on and now re-Christened Cranfield University; the College main hall is the setting for another mission by Sgt Pepper and the regiment into the darker reaches of rural Bedfordshire.

This is not quite Derek Horsler's cup of tea. A cultural, gentle man, Derek would hardly relish the idea of his ex-star pupil degrading himself in such a manner. Anne and I owe Derek a great deal, not least bringing us together in the cast of *Billy Liar* in which I played Billy and she played my mother, a role she claims to have reluctantly repeated in the domestic sense ever since. Derek directed the school plays at Icknield High School in Luton alongside Marion Dunn, a stern-looking schoolma'am who proved to have a far more generous and humorous nature than most pupils could ever imagine.

Since my family caught the bug for promoting Sgt Pepper, relatives and old acquaintances have found themselves witnessing a performance by a local lad they last saw onstage over twenty five years ago. Offstage, they immediately recognise Anne but it takes them awhile to work out the bald bloke next to her. The shoulder-length wig soon gives the game away.

The University hall is well furnished and ideal for a cabaret-style show. My mum Pauline, in her Cameron Macintosh capacity has had to fight off local residents from Silsoe who, having heard about our previous appearance last November, are desperately pleading with her to exceed the 200 capacity. The local branch of the Motor Neurone Association have hijacked the evening as a fund-raiser and on this occasion extended family and invited guests are considerably outnumbered.

Silsoe, to use estate agents' parlance, is a "highly desirable" village between Luton and Bedford. Wrest Park, the village's major attraction, hikes up house prices in an area already attractive to the moneyed London commuter. My brother Hugh and his wife Gill recently moved from suburban Luton to the village of Maulden, a little further along the A6. Maulden has the distinction of being the site of the infamous murder after which Hanratty was sent to the gallows on the basis of long-debated police evidence. Bedfordshire is a small county and as we leave the M1, Anne provides the children with the usual tourist guide of the villages she remembers from her childhood, before her parents uprooted to Luton. This brings the predictable groans of despair from the back seat.

Despite a slow start and gatecrashers further diminishing the less than generous buffet, the evening proves a memorable end to Steve's tenure as bass player with the band. He requests we do "Drive My Car" as the final encore and afterwards we present him with a framed photo of us in full swing. Before opening the wrapper, Steve anticipates that it's a picture of Mike, naked. Even though he's joining The Skooters we could never do that to him. We will miss him as a musician and a friend, a point I make in my brief farewell from the stage. Steve is not one to show his emotions but tonight back in the dressing room (for "dressing room" read:

"disabled toilet") his reaction suggests he might just miss us too.

Guest rooms are available at the university for the band but Steve has decided to make a clean break after the show. With Tom at home enjoying the Freedom of Frome, the rest of my family and I spend the night at Hugh's.

May 2nd

A lunchtime party at Hugh and Gill's to celebrate son Jamie's fourth birthday. It's a rare opportunity for the family to get together. Mum's looking a bit knackered and deflated after setting up last night's do. Her younger sister Denise, far too close to my age for me to seriously consider as an Auntie, was also involved in the promotion and is now unwinding with a customary beer and publicly proclaiming her secret desire to try cannabis. Like a true sixties generation parent, she still awaits her daughter Zoe's approval. Hugh's eldest daughter Megan, meanwhile, plays host to her cousins and convinces me that a theatrical gene courses through the family.

Paul, our brother, arrives with Nicola and their children Matthew, Emma and Jack. Paul and Hugh are twins. Six years my junior, both have made a very comfortable living in the used car business. Hugh is the more laid back and seemingly responsible. Paul always has been the more impulsive, egotistical and generally barmy of the two, though the roles do tend to swap from time to time. Last night Paul gave every appearance of wishing he was up there, belting out "Get Back". He saves his vocal talents however, for the showrooms and auctions of the used car trade, where he can charm the best prices from buyers and sellers alike. Hugh drifted into the business after a few jobs and a spell with Camp America. They have one 'O' Level between them, though Hugh really should have added to his singular contribution. Hugh is outgoing and friendly but with a hidden, sensitive side. Paul's emotions are never far from the surface. He is outrageous in his humour and always "up for the crack". The band, having again encountered "Del Boy" Dimery, with his wide-boy patter and desire to impress on them jokes he can barely remember, are convinced that one of us must have been adopted.

Hugh and Paul share a close but frequently conflicting relationship. The bond was best exemplified when, during their late teens Hugh, in attendance at a Luton Town match, joined in the chorus of derisory cheering that greeted a scuffle at the opposition end. Two spectators were being forcibly removed by the police from the terrace. As they were frogmarched towards the players tunnel, Hugh's amusement turned to dismay as the dark haired, stockier of the two came into closer view. Why Paul should seriously wish to spend the afternoon caged up with two thousand hostile hooligans from Brighton and Hove Albion was beyond anyone's comprehension. Despite his disapproval, Hugh waited patiently at the police station for two hours to ensure our parents escaped the ignominy of having to collect their errant son.

Paul shares a particularly fond relationship with Ivy, our 92 year-old grandmother. Even Ivy says she enjoyed last night's do although it's hard to tell as she didn't dance much.

May 5ᵗʰ - Hello Goodbye...

Mike phones:

"Martin, are you busy tonight? Only, I think I need to come round for a chat."

Déjà vu occurs. John has already tipped me off that Mike is finding it hard to sustain our schedule. On Saturday he arrived only twenty minutes before curtain up. In addition to his teaching and theatre work, Mike is also a professional photographer and was busy covering a wedding in Bath. Many more weddings threaten to compromise his availability in the summer.

Mike's talent for the visual and theatrical has played a major part in the band's stage presentation. Seeking out and adapting military uniforms to look like the Sgt Pepper drawing on the original album pull out, gave the musicians much more impact than the previous printed T-shirt ensemble. Although onstage we liken the lads to the Salvation Army, they blend in well against the vivid, full-length coats worn by the front line. All except Lester that is, who with his peaked cap pulled down over his eyes and his distinctive profile, is off-puttingly reminiscent of Blakey in *On the Buses*. As well as costume, the use of projectors, a proper lighting rig and some decidedly dodgy palm-trees, have all been down to Mike's dramatic intuition.

Mike was stage director of the original *All You Need is Love* production in 1995. I directed the music in what was to be my farewell show at Frome College. Many of the original cast, and almost the entire band with the notable exception of Steve, were not available for the revival tour of Germany and the Czech Republic in '96. Fortunately, the delightfully long summer holiday at Millfield meant I was free to join the end of term trip, along with Anne (who looked after the costume wardrobe) and the children. A new band was built around Steve that meant another six-month rehearsal schedule. I slightly resented this, believing some of the original musicians had dropped out due to a needless vendetta that came about after frictions between Mike and themselves when he directed the local pantomime at The Merlin. Fortunately I have an aversion to cross-dressing and so have never been involved in the panto. As it turned out, the similarity in age and interests meant Rob, Tony and Lester fitted in perfectly, making the extra rehearsals an enjoyable necessity.

Nigel Mintram, also a College teacher and talented performer, had originally played Ringo, bearing a remarkable similarity to Barry Wom, the pastiche of Mr. Starr in the TV show *The Rutles*. Mike felt he could fit Nigel's shoes for the revival and so it proved. The Ringo role carried much of the comic narration but was not as crucial to the vocal sound.

Incorporating Mike into the line-up after *All You Need is Love* required a certain amount of creative thinking and he has always been appreciative of the fact that we treated him as an equal partner. His contribution to the Dart Board Band has not been dissimilar to Ringo's in The Beatles. Ringo was often underestimated as a drummer. It is not until you attempt to reproduce The Beatles sound that you appreciate the distinctive but understated style of percussion. Listen to the phrasing on "A Day in the Life" or the persistent roll through "Get Back" and you can hear exactly how the drums give the music momentum. Many of The Beatles early rock numbers like "A Hard Days Night", or "I Saw Her Standing There" are not fast and furious but steady and catchy, sustained by the clever rhythmic awareness of Ringo alongside Paul McCartney's inventive bass lines. We also may have underestimated Mike's harmonies and the power he gave to sing-a-long choruses like "All You Need is Love" and "Hello Goodbye". It was perhaps only when he missed the odd gig that we really appreciated his contribution.

In theatre presentations we wrote in a number of gags in which we mention The Beatles solo work. The best example of solo material that Ringo Starr (or Bingo Card as we call him) could come up with was *Thomas the Tank Engine*. To this purpose we wrote Bingo a sketch at the beginning of the second half in which he reads a send-up of the children's story before belatedly realising that John and Paul have doctored the Reverend Awdry's naive narrative about macho male engines pulling silly, giggly female trucks. The script is full of Benny Hill type innuendoes, making perverse reference to "ramming the trucks in the buffers" and "Thomas's funnel being polished with a brillo pad." To be honest, John and I had our doubts as to whether the audience would find this "Carry-On Thomas" material funny. Mike managed to affect that droll mock-sincerity that typified Ringo's character in the films and the audiences fell for it. Except on one occasion, that is. We were playing in front of a school audience at Millfield in what is archaically known as a "School Hop". The kids were very noisy and over-reacted to everything, behaving like prisoners on the first night of parole. We politely suggested to Mike that the *Thomas the Tank Engine* section should be cut, but he insisted on giving it a try, saying that we can always interrupt him if the story begins to labour. As Mike went through the motions, the catcalls and whistles grew in volume. I was anxious to bail him out but John kept saying, "No, no, he's alright. They'll calm down in a minute." Eventually I insisted we went on to prevent Mike's further humiliation. It seemed to me John was taking perverse pleasure in watching Mike wrestle with the unseemly mob. It wasn't until after the show that I realised that John had positioned himself in the wings out of view of the forestage and unlike myself, was oblivious to the fact that Mike was being heavily pelted with the rolled up remnants of several school exercise books.

Mike, as anticipated, has decided to leave. He is eager to explain his conflicting commitments and also the feeling that with Steve being replaced by John and my decision to play guitar, he is going to look a little out of place onstage. I assure him that we would have expanded his role accordingly but we both know the integrity of his opinion. Mike has clearly thought the matter through. We were planning to use his PA system instead of Steve's for which we would have continued to pay a nominal hire charge of ten pounds per performance. Mike suggests instead that we buy the system from him in instalments. He will also give us the lighting he provided on a loan basis. He even wants to sign

Being John Lennon

off by magnanimously taking publicity photos of the new line-up for our future use.

While it will be possible for Lester and Stuart to take on Mike's vocals, we must remind ourselves not to sacrifice the pastiche-style often prompted by Mike's character that has helped distinguish our act from most other Beatles tributes.

In less than a year, Alex has withdrawn to concentrate on his studies; Tony has handed back the drum seat to Stuart who was in the original *All You Need is Love*; Steve has ski-daddled to The Skooters and now Mike has hung up his wig. While the simplicity of transporting a five-piece band and the knowledge of a larger share of the purse are alluring compensations, we must now prove we can still deliver the same quality to those who have booked our services through-out the summer. On Tuesday we are to break the habit of a lifetime and start rehearsing again.

May 11th

Full rehearsal: John is surprisingly confident and has been working hard at the bass lines. John has many talents, as a singer, comedy performer and writer of sketches and songs. He was once dubbed "Ton-up Freeman" in bold headlines on the back page of the *Western Daily Press*. This was not some kind of sleaze scandal of Bill Wyman proportions but one of several centuries scored as Frome's number one bats-man. Without doubt, John could have played cricket and other sports at a much higher level. He's far and away the most versatile person I've ever known. This is why I'd never regarded him as a virtuoso bass player, believing nobody has a right to be that talented. Years of playing week-in week-out with The Havana Fireflies however, have given him a depth of instrumental experience comparable to any of us. While he may not be another Jack Bruce, his fingers are flying up the fretboard with considerable dexterity while he manages with remarkable co-ordination, to sing the lead vocal on "Lady Madonna". The best compliment any of us can pay him is that at times, we forgot it wasn't Steve.

22nd May

A fund-raiser in the village hall at Beckington is the ideal way to break in the new line-up. Oddly enough, my first visit to the hall which is only a couple of miles north of Frome, was last Sunday to see a public rehearsal by the re-formed seventies folk-rock band, Stackridge. I hadn't realised their violinist was Mike Evans, who I know from teaching his talented daughter Ruth at Frome College. Mike turned up in a country trio to play in a line dance act I'd booked for the Millfield Holiday Village two years ago and is now very much the typical jobbing musician.

Mike lives in Beckington which is why this unlikely venue provided Stackridge with a warm-up for their forthcoming come-back tour. Their style is usually described as "whimsical" in the music press, borne out by songs with titles like "Syracuse the Elephant". I knew little of the band in my youth, wrongly attributing them as heavy metal. Possibly I mistook the name to connote a wall of speaker stacks. They are infact, a very subtle, clever and intelligent group of musicians that continue to appeal to the aging hippie generation. The concert was informal but impressive; the technical musicianship enviable and the songs melodic and provocative.

Freeman's bass playing debut day cannot get much worse given that he supports Newcastle who feebly capitulated this afternoon to Manchester United in the FA Cup Final. He seems very philosophical and keen to get on with the job. It is a long time since any of us felt more than a slight twinge of apprehension prior to a gig. Tonight we could re-stock a butterfly farm. There is considerable curiosity as to whether we can pull it off without Steve and Mike. Along with a larger than usual turn out of band wives, Tony Stockley calls in to checkout the new sound in view of his future deps for Stuart. Mike and Viv Walker also arrive in time for the second half. Mike's appearance gives us the opportunity to call him up to the stage for a farewell rendition of "Yellow Submarine". We then present him the now customary Sgt Pepper retirement gift of a framed photo of the band and a *Thomas the Tank Engine* card addressed to "The Fat Controller".

John manages to get through the entire show with hardly a dropped note and seems to be alive with adrenaline. He contributes even more chirpy banter than ever and has retained most of his solo singing despite earlier reservations. Music stands onstage do not seem inappropriate in a Victorian brass band setting and so John is able to read off cue sheets the songs that are hardest to remember. We were all rather too dependent on music stands in the early shows, even reading dialogue off them in "All You Need is Love". On the last night of the original production in the Ecos Amphitheatre, Frome, a gust of wind left John speechless as it carried his script into the adjoining car park. The ensuing ad-libbed dialogue was, as it happened, far funnier than anything we'd penned in advance.

Learning Beatles tunes is not easy. The genius of Lennon and McCartney's melodies lies in their tendency to be simple and memorable without being obvious. Even the early songs are far from predictable. The pattern of most pop songs follow a familiar formula. For instance, a reasonably experienced guitarist can work out the chords for an Oasis song like "Wonderwall" in about five minutes. No... make that two minutes. The Beatles' songs however, utilise a range of major and minor chords which owe as much to stage musical melodies as early rock'n' roll. Listen to McCartney singing "Till There Was You" from *The Music Man* then imagine the verse of "She Loves You" slowed down with the same plaintive feel and the song would not be out of place in a fifties Broadway show. As we play "She Loves You" I find myself looking across to Lester to check that there really is a C minor on "And with a love like that". It fits perfectly of course but is quite an unexpected progression in a pop song. "She Loves You", far from being an early sketch in The Beatles colourful collection, is in many respects a masterpiece of tone and construction.

My own contribution on guitar was far less significant. It seemed more important for me to carry the show unhindered from glancing down at the music stand and risk errors. Keeping the volume discreetly low, I managed to keep most mistakes under wraps whilst contributing quite effectively in songs like "We Can Work it Out" where a simple, acoustic rhythm sustains throughout. The old Hofner Verithin gave the right sixties tone but recent renovations have done little to improve its inclination to lose tuning or buzz like a Black and Decker power drill, if not handled with reverence.

Anne, who has earned the reputation of being an honest, if undiplomatic critic, appears backstage after the show. A unanimous chorus of "Oh, here we go!" greets her arrival.

"No!" she says in her assertive pseudo-Cockney. "I thought it was brilliant!"

A slight pause follows as we await further qualification. "Is that it?" says Rob.

"Well..." says Anne trying hard now to act to type. "Your guitar was a bit loud Lester. And John's coat could do with a bloody good wash."

The oracle hath spoken.

"If that was the best Anne could come up with, we can't have been bad," says Lester.

And we weren't. The harmonies from Lester and Stuart need a bit more confidence but that should come with practice. Mike and Tony are both complimentary but clearly

Being John Lennon

more aware of the areas that need tightening up. The punters as ever, suspended disbelief perhaps a fraction more than usual but didn't take long for them to hit the dance floor.

May 24th

Solo appearance in a charity show at the Meyer Theatre, Millfield. I am determined not to perform anything by The Beatles. Having taken a minute or two to actually work out "Wonderwall" I decide to do a one-man Oasis tribute. Wearing my John Lennon sunglasses, woolly hat pulled low to hide balding eyebrows and feet splayed out like Chaplin, I loaf on as Liam Gallagher giving the audience the usual platitudes about it being "really mad for it... like". But my broad Mancunian slips, not unnaturally, into Lennonesque Liverpool. An easy-to-please school audience respond with the expected (if patronising) enthusiasm at discovering a teacher who has not only heard of Oasis but can even play one of their songs. "Peggy Sue" and "I'm A Believer" enable me to revert to type and finish with tunes that truly reflect my age.

May 28th

We have an Olympic-sized swimming pool at Millfield. Never has it been put to more appalling use than in this end-of-half-term fundraiser. For no better purpose than helping to subsidise the mostly over-privileged girls hockey team tour of Bermuda, I have been duped into appearing along with nine other colleagues of assorted weight, size and talent in a "Man Oh Man" male beauty competition. After describing myself in no more than three words ("Bald But Beautiful" if you must know), I am selected for the final eliminator in which it's "shirts off, trunks on and please copy the following fitness routine to music" – as demonstrated by weights instructor and general brick-shithouse, Kev Simmons. Kev manages to exhaust the pathetic finalists before forcing our puce and puny bodies through the ritual humiliation of attempting to display muscles that have atrophied long before they ever put to serious use. Next to the bulging Kev, I must resemble the last turkey in the shop. Given the distinctly ironic nature of the competition, I'm not sure whether winning third place has enhanced or diminished my credibility. I suspect the latter.

May 29th

Hanbury Manor will be hosting the English Open Golf Tournament next week. The smooth texture of the brick suggests the Manor House was built more recently than I imagined. Closer inspection reveals it is hideously over-extended from its historic core to form an elaborate golf and country club complex. Our hired mini-bus with its bright red livery proclaiming "Frome Self-Drive" looks somewhat incongruous parked outside the main entrance, obscuring from passing view the impressive line-up of Ferraris and Aston Martins which frame an old, white Bentley convertible wedding car. This genteel country estate near Ware has clearly become a refuge for the pretentious and vulgar. The ideal setting infact, for Gazza's over-hyped wedding a few years ago.

The day begins with collecting the mini-bus. The bus is one of a fleet owned by a Frome family firm whose rates are very reasonable. This is probably because they use most of a public lay-by as their personal car park. Gathered around the desk in their tiny office with cups of tea and the smell of recently devoured bacon lingering in the air, "mother" deals with our enquiry with all the tact and efficiency she can muster after creating a fitting mid-morning snack for her chaps.

"What mini-bus? Which name? On what chart? Where's me glasses? Oh you're Mr. Davey. Going to Burnham with the pensioners... no? Dimery? I can't see it here... Oh, there you are. Yes, we need him back by eight o'clock tomorrow morning." (Inanimate objects are always "him" or "her" in Somerset).

As I'd visited the company no less than three times to view and book one of their vehicles, during which time no end of unhelpful confusion had taken place, my irritation at this further incompetence cannot be disguised.

"When I booked this vehicle over a month ago you informed me that it was a twenty-four hour hire and that we could return it before mid-day," I pontificate. "I confirmed this with you by calling in last week. We will not be returning from the South East until four o'clock tomorrow morning and now you're suggesting I have to get up at seven thirty because you've booked it out to someone else."

"Well, you should have said," replies mother.

"I did... twice."

"I (sic) tell you what," this is "father" intervening, "you leave it outside your house in the morning with the key on the passenger side front wheel and we'll pick 'im up."

After trying to explain where I live in words of not more than one syllable, Rob suggests they pick it up from his house. An admirable solution until mother confuses the issue with a less than complete interpretation of local geography.

Eldest son escorts me to the mini-bus to show me around. He checks the oil.

"He's a bit low. I'll fill him up."

"Is there an oil leak?" I enquire with thinly disguised suspicion.

"No, no. Someone left the dip-stick out, that's all. Engine gets a bit messy that way."

I clamber aboard, having almost snapped off all my finger nails trying to open the door.

"He's a bit tight," says eldest son, helpfully.

I can see why they are unconcerned by the possibility of all our heavy gear resting on their seats or some passing stranger stealing the bus from Rob's drive. Judging from the interior smell, the vehicle had recently returned from taking a party of Young Smokers to a beer festival close to a fish factory in Stinkley-on-Sea.

"Sorry. Our barrel's run out," says eldest son on his return. "Do you think you could put in a litre of oil when you fill her up?"

Desperate to get on the road, I agree.

He gives me three pounds, saying, "That should cover it."

I start the bus up, rev the engine, find the gear and go to check the rear view mirror. It has fallen off. Undaunted, I sluggishly pull out in front of an oncoming lorry and head for the nearest petrol station. The oil costs £4.25.

Early afternoon... and as I begin picking up the band, a thunderstorm gathers momentum. The sky above Frome is purple and so overcast that the street lights have come on. Tony Stockley is sitting in for Stuart on this gig and by the time we reach his house in Westbury the storm has broken violently. We desperately try to squeeze his drum kit into what space is left on the bus whilst illegally parked and with rain lashing in through the open doors and onto the equipment. Tony's wife Sally looks on in amusement from the front window. We head out across Salisbury Plain where the open skyline reveals the sheer magnitude of the storm. I was half expecting to be confronted the Four Horsemen of the Apocalypse en-route, but rather sensibly they had decided the weather was a little too inclement. Whilst cars struggle through floodwater knee-deep, we are actually rather grateful to be in a high vehicle. At one point the wash from a passing truck created a wave of surf that almost engendered a medley of Beach Boys favourites. At least it would have done, had not Lester and John fallen asleep almost from the moment we left Tony's. It is extraordinary how these two have the capacity to "drop-off" in a vehicle. The reluctance of Rob and I to allow them to take the wheel has been borne-out. Tony, increasingly more cramped as dozing arms, legs and buttocks are spread across him, clambers in the front for refuge.

The receptionist at Hanbury Manor is in no hurry to get our imposing vehicle moved from his forecourt. We finally decide to locate the hall entrance for ourselves as no member of staff seems willing to help. On arriving at the rear of the reception hall, we are politely informed by the Senior Steward/ Head Waiter (or whatever he's called) that we can't set up until after the speeches. With a pianist playing a grand piano, a DJ and ourselves all booked to appear on the same stage area, there is clearly an element of overkill. We eventually persuade the organisers that if we don't set up around their elegant but obstructive baby-grand, there won't be time for more than half an hour of disco and band.

Having set up, we then adjourn with our co-operative DJ friend to whatever room the management can find for us to rest and change. While the room is very pleasant, no thought has been given to the needs of the entertainers and so chairs have become an optional luxury. We make enquiries to find out where we are to eat. Bill and Yvonne (the happy couple) have arranged for us to be fed and we are naturally, fairly ravenous by mid-evening. We are instructed to go to the club restaurant to be greeted with horror by the Germanic Head Waiter who politely but firmly informs us that we are improperly dressed.

"It is not my fault, you understand," he asserts. "It is ze rules of ze house. I personally do not make ze rules. The dress code is no jeans you see... und ties. You must have a tie. Trainers too are verboten. It is unfortunate... but they are not my rules."

I am sorely tempted to say, "Yes, of course, I see you are only obeying orders," but resist.

Even when we politely enquire as to where we might be fed, he continues to apologise and deny responsibility. As Mike the DJ, Tony and I are all ageing skinheads, perhaps he fears some kind of racist bovver. Since Manchester United beat Bayern Munich in the European Cup Final on Wednesday, we decide to let him off with an insubordinate gloat.

We are informed that the food will be brought down to our room and we may select from "ze range of sandviches". Naturally we choose the Hanbury Club Sandwich which defies its classification, is highly expensive and proves a substantial meal. Inevitably it takes half-an-hour for a waiter to collect our order and a further half-hour or more for the sandwiches to arrive, by which time we have, at least, been provided with chairs on which to sit. A trolley skids through the door, powerfully pushed by a young waiter who rapidly retreats before it has come to rest, as if delivering half a dozen primed hand-grenades.

He has obviously been forewarned by the Head Waiter: "Your mission is to infiltrate ze skinhead rock band mit die club sandwiches. Do not loiter in zer company. If zey question you... remember... you are only obeying orders."

Fifty minutes on, the drinks have yet to arrive. Tony, a veteran of cruise liners and hotels, picks up the internal phone and demands service. The drinks duly appear. Problems with the pump, apparently. Hanbury Manor staff are obviously trained in the art of excuse management. Presumably Nick Faldo, Greg Norman and Sevvy can look forward to cataloguing the excuses next week. Freeman though, is a little more impressed, having met Warren Barton, the Newcastle full back, whilst snooping around the Health Club.

We eventually get on at about 10.30 for a one hour thrash. My voice is rather tired and my throat dry. We are all squeaking a bit on the high notes, probably a result of the carbon monoxide leakage from the mini-bus exhausts. Some of us are well tanked up by the time we get on and hit the set at lightening pace, testing John's fingering more than a multiple hire in a Bangkok brothel.

Bill and Yvonne give their thanks. We privately feel that we haven't lived up to their expectations when they booked us after the Hertfordshire Golf Club do.

"You guys certainly get them up dancing, don't you?" says Bill.

We certainly do – but tonight they were doing the twist at such velocity there was a risk of mass hip dislocations. Part of the problem seems to be having John in the front line with his bass cabinet too far away from the drummer. Tony, having not played with us for awhile has to guess at the pace, instead of taking his cue from John. We decide in future to keep physically closer onstage. It also helps me when singing, to be within natural earshot of John on the close harmonies. We may have to sacrifice The Beatles distinctive onstage shape in order to recover our "tight" sound.

Bill's mate seemed impressed anyway, proudly boasting about some of the tribute bands he had booked for his local rugby club.

"You should see the Queen tribute," he says in his upmarket cockney accent. "The fella who done Freddie Mercury... he was the business. Looked the dead spit. Rolled up in an open top BMW, shirt undone, medallion, sunglasses, the lot. Real star quality. Got the audience going from the start. Right on top of these speakers he was. Bloody brilliant. Couldn't sing though."

Freddie of course, had a voice that would make larks drop off their perch in envy. Maybe we're doing it all wrong. Perhaps we should arrive in a stretch limo, go in for a new wardrobe of costumes and play like a garage band. Bill's mate then tells me he's booked The Bandit Beatles in the Autumn.

"What's that? The Arse-Bandit Beatles?" Lester quickly responds.

"I bet you paid a lot for them," I suggest.

He proudly pronounces the cost. Bill, listening in, suddenly looks like a man who has just got the bargain of the century.

"You should have booked us," I reply. "You might have saved yourself a grand."

Bill's mate gives me a knowing shrug and I depart.

As Tony Stockley points out in the bus: "You can only be so good at this game. One good Beatles tribute is going to sound the same as any other. What's more, we use live keyboards and no backing tapes. Why the hell are people prepared to pay so much for less?"

I was beginning to think we were doing rather well at this business but like the journey back to Frome, there's still a bloody long way to go.

The Idiot's Guide... No: 5
Sgt Pepper's Lonely Hearts Club Band

When Steve and Mike left the band, the song that should have been our signature tune suddenly became a problem. We always opened the show with the "Sgt Pepper" song, allowing the opening riff to go round a few times as Mike, John and myself made a grand entrance. With John and I both instrumentalists, this was no longer possible. The other problem with the song is the delicate mix on the record which is hard to capture onstage.

Thanks to greatly enhanced and more subtle amplification, plus the advantage of listening to Beatles recordings through the medium of CD (the clarity of which enables parts to be more faithfully recreated), some Beatles tribute bands can sound more like the early Beatles in concert than could The Beatles themselves. When The Beatles retired from live performance and utilised developing studio technology of mixing and over-dubbing however, they left most cover bands behind. The fact that the sophisticated *Sgt Pepper's Lonely Hearts Club Band* album was recorded on only a four track machine further illustrates George Martin's astonishing talent as a producer and arranger.

The opening track "Sgt Pepper" emerges from the sounds of an orchestra tuning up against audience chatter. It is a fairly orthodox pop song in structure with McCartney's high, Little Richard type vocal and the guitar fills lending it a rock'n'roll edge. The song plods quite slowly however, the drums are fairly mute and so it eases seamlessly into the clever brass band instrumental. In live performance though, put a drum kit in a space, whether it be a pub skittle alley in Dorset or Wembley Arena and the sound will resonate and carry. This in turn determines the volume of the other instruments. The raunchy but dampened sound of the lead guitar becomes simply raunchy. Add to that the adrenaline of live performance and the tendency to play a little faster than the record (which I note, was also true of The Beatles) and you have a more urgent, energetic but less controlled sound.

It is easy to overplay the title song of *Sgt Pepper*. The new line up was certainly less comfortable with the number and my own guitar chords were cluttering the mix. We now save "Sgt Pepper" as an encore, doing a hybrid arrangement incorporating the lyrics and feel of the album's reprise version.

When Paul McCartney invented Sgt Pepper's Lonely Hearts Club Band he was marking the transition from the moptops to mavericks, from entertainers to composers. *Revolver* had already begun the transition, combining a simple sing-along like "Yellow Submarine" with the classical "Eleanor Rigby"; contrasting George's pop reggae of "Taxman" with John's ground breaking mantra "Tomorrow Never Knows". The *Pepper* album though, rarely reverts to the accepted pop-rock idiom. It is by turns, psychedelic, ballad style, Music Hall and (with "A Day in the Life") almost symphonic.

The *Sgt Pepper* concept also served to create a new image for The Beatles. They had outgrown live performance and matured into four individuals changed by drugs, by endless touring, by social influence and by their own eminence as spokesmen for modern youth. Sgt Pepper's band was just the kind of arty, retro and tongue-in-cheek persona for Lennon to be able to launch his (then unflattering) pebble glasses on the world. These were grown men with serious moustaches and hair layered down into Victorian sideburns. They were removing themselves one step from The Beatles we had all grown to know and love. They were now beginning to develop distinctively different writing styles. Their individuality is marked by the fact that the *Sgt Pepper* cover represents the last time we see John, Paul, George and Ringo in matching uniforms.

What better image for a bunch of has-been ageing tribute performers to adopt than Sgt Pepper's band? The uniforms conveniently hide bulging waist lines and the wigs conceal receding hairlines. A liberal use of Lennon shades by all members of the band further reduces the need to be a "look-a-like." As Sgt Pepper's Lonely Hearts Club Band was one step removed from The Beatles, so Sgt Pepper's Only Dart Board Band could be a few steps further behind. It's rather like what theatre directors devoted to Bertolt Brecht call "alienation". It helps distance the audience from the expectation that they are going to see an exact (and impossible) replica of the originals and so allows us a little more scope for interpretation and self-deprecating humour.

Brecht and The Beatles? This is beginning to sound like a university thesis... I do apologise.

June

June 4th

I can't seem to let a holiday go by without spending a disproportionate amount of time on the phone begging for bookings. It really is no better than selling double-glazing. Experience in theatre management has taught me how tedious it is receiving calls from companies and performers, desperate to fill another date in the interminable diary.

The large majority of our bookings come from regular sources or from people actually seeing our show. New venues are always important if the act is to move on but finding an eager promoter can take five failed calls before finally speaking to the person in charge. Bearing in mind that probably only one in seven or eight venues are likely to show any genuine interest, it sometimes takes thirty five calls or more to secure one booking in a reasonable venue. Sending publicity materials in advance is usually a waste of time as careers officers have obviously been trained to advise anyone suffering a reading disorder to become a music promoter. I recently mailed out some thirty schools with theatres presuming that it was not a market of which many bands were aware. So far I have had one return call requesting further details. With videos and hand-outs sent on, I am banking on this venue just to recover overheads on marketing.

A promoter, after initial enthusiasm, has failed to get us a regular pitch at the new cabaret club opening in Bristol on account of the owner preferring a traditional "mop tops" type Beatle tribute. I expect he'll end up paying about twice our normal fee to back his judgement, before rapidly going bankrupt. Bristol is our nearest major city and we're keen to raise our profile in the more "serious" rock venues.

The promoter at a major Bristol pub venue The Fleece and Firkin, sounds interested. It is gratifying to know he has heard of us.

"Send the video but mark it 'Beatles' so I'll be able to pick it out from all the other crap I receive," he requests.

"Don't worry," I reply. "I'll mark it 'Beatles Crap'."

Of course, no amount of crap can guarantee a good fee and some of the most respected clubs on the circuit offer the worst deals, particularly in London, where bands are desperate for the exposure. Here we find ourselves in a quandary. With fees for weddings and events at up-market venues now in the "respectable though not lucrative" category, should we be bothering with token payments to play sleazy bars?

With the garage cluttered full of PA and lighting, my study bursting with posters and publicity; with debts to pay off on both the above and the new line-up still bedding-in, the Dart Board Band suddenly seems less of an escape and more of a committal. The honeymoon, after four years, is belatedly but inevitably, over.

It is still pleasing though, to see our name headlining posters on two forthcoming outdoor events and featuring in the Bath Festival brochure. June and July provide us with a heavy sequence of high-pressure gigs. If we reach our August break feeling positive and enthusiastic about the new line-up and the diary bulging with Autumn offers, then all will be well. If not...

June 7th

Return to work to receive call from St. Edward's School, Oxford, booking us for their Christmas concert. Apparently, they run one of the biggest concert halls in the city. Hope springs eternal.

June 10th

I have finally come to terms with my problem. The long period of denial is over. I have signed myself in to The Priory clinic. The setting is very much like Hanbury Manor but the staff are a little more respectful. I lodge in a simple but pleasant room next to Lenny Henry. Tara Palmer-Tomkinson fleets around the corridors like Lady Macbeth doing odd things with talcum powder. Paul Merson is just up the passage but Paul Merton nowhere to be seen, which is strange because his mother, Mrs Merton, is a regular visitor. Rumour has it that Gazza has just checked in again, confusing The Priory with Hanbury Manor Country Club. Cocaine, it seems has been my undoing, leading to the insatiable desire for sex. Given the shortage of dwarf women who actually own a wet suit, I was finally persuaded to seek a cure after resorting to sexual gratification with a well-oiled pig wearing a balacalava.

The above is, of course, a vain attempt to compensate for this diary's lack of sex and drugs which would normally be the mainstay of the archetypal rock biography. The late nights can sometimes be an immense irritation to our partners but none of us gives them anything to worry about. If you saw us in the flesh, you'd probably realise why.

I now find myself drawn even closer to convention today when quite unexpectedly being offered the post of Head of House at Millfield. The school is almost the biggest boarding institution in the country but I have avoided the temptation to become a boarding houseparent, knowing the conflicts this would create with my family, my theatre post and not least, the band. Being in charge of one of seven Day Houses for non-boarders is an ideal and convenient promotion. Accepting the post effectively ties me to Millfield in the immediate future and makes me part of the establishment. The Day Houses take on the names of their managers and so the birth of "Dimery House" has given rise to much amusement in my family. I suppose I'd better postpone the long awaited flirtation with heroin addiction for a while longer.

June 11th

As we drive through a leafy avenue full of respectable looking hotels, I begin to imagine that the Central Hotel in Poole might not, for once, be the usual down-at-heel rock venue we anticipate. Turning the corner however, I am quickly restored to reality. Set amongst a busy district of Edwardian terraces at the back of town, the Central is an old hotel and pub that probably aspired to respectability in the 1930s. One can imagine a pre-war couple stepping out from the Central after a simple but filling steak-and-kidney suet supper, to take the short tram-ride to view the harbour sunset. He, an undermanager at a brass fittings factory in Slough, would be wearing an ensemble which was daringly close to casual for the time: A dog-tooth checked jacket with separate beige Oxford bags and clean socks, visible through brown leather sandals. A collar and tie would not be abandoned for fear of being mistaken for a "lesser class of person" and the sandals would be polished as dutifully as if they were brogues. In fact, the shine on the sandals would only be offset by the setting sun glistening on his well scrubbed neck, closely shaved cheeks and the top of his sunburned bald head, as slippery as a Brylcreemed bowling ball. The good lady wife would be wearing her loud, floral dress, a fake-pearl necklace with matching handbag and high heels. A white cardigan "in case it turns chilly" would be draped across her shoulders. They would step out to the front with all the aplomb of the Prince of Wales and "that American woman," Mrs Simpson. (Wallace, that is, not Marge.) I think I may have almost described my grandparents.

Anyway, what Ivy and Ted (as they shall be named) would think of the Central now, I don't know, but I doubt that they would be impressed by the threadbare carpets and surly saloon-bar regulars. What they might make of the long-haired lads with their obscene T-shirts and baggy denims doesn't really bare thinking about. The boys are a friendly bunch though, eager to arrive early enough to hear the soundcheck.

Of course double-yellow lines make parking and unloading problematic, coupled with the fact that the performing area is up two flights of narrow stairs. In this function room an effort has been made to provide a stage and dress it with a wonderfully tasteless mock-Greek cyclorama. Oddly enough, the place rather grows on you. It has a lived-in and comfortable feel.

Music is now the Central's speciality. Bands play most nights of the week and the management helps publish a leaflet called *Livewire* which lists music at venues throughout the Bournemouth and Poole region. It seems the Central is the local "in" venue and as such offers no guaranteed fee but gives the door-take to the band. This puts an onus on Anne to turn up to sell tickets.

My earlier fears of an audience in single figures are unfounded. Only forty turn up in total but they make their presence felt. The early arrivals are very drunk by the second half and calling out requests for "Helter Skelter", "Happiness is a Warm Gun", "Why Don't We Do It in the Road?" and other drug-induced rants from the *White Album*. John strings them along with the suggestion that the only one we know on the *White Album* is "Revolution No 9". This backfires badly as they actually believe him and start looking forward to it. The lads become ecstatic with delight when we hit them with "Revolution" and "Back in the USSR" and kneel before a bemused Lester in worshipful "we're not worthy" fashion, during his raunchy guitar breaks. This is a reaction he rarely receives in his role as deputy projectionist from audiences at the local Frome fleapit.

The gig proves something of a bench-mark. It is only the third since John took over on bass and to our collective surprise his confidence has grown greatly since the last show. A rehearsal earlier in the week seems to have ironed out a few creases and backing vocals too are working well. The set is almost as tight and confident as in Steve's day. For John the evening is slightly tarnished by the encore. A few pints for the worse, Lester exits off-stage right on the final beat of "Twist and Shout", desperate to shower the Armitage Shanks. With the audience bellowing for an encore, Rob saves our blushes by suggesting "Let it Be" which, he calculates, will give Lester ample time to attend to his toilet before making a timely entrance on the guitar solo. He begins playing the opening piano chords when John, who has discreetly tried to stop us, finally blurts out that he doesn't know the song. I had forgotten that he'd left this one off his "urgent" list but I insist we continue in the hope he will pick it up. John covers his tracks admirably but is understandably pissed off after the show at having his hard work undermined. I rather abruptly point out that we were in grave danger of "looking like a bunch of twats" if we simply did nothing. Lester, at this time, is skulking around the sizeable dressing room a little sheepishly.

The only other blot on the performance was the persistent snap, crackle and pop of my Hofner Verithin. I decide to forego the classic look on our next gig in favour of a guitar that doesn't actually sound like an anus-rupturing fart.

We belatedly discover that rooms are available at the Central at little charge, should we wish to stay. Working on

Saturday morning once again prevents this pleasant alternative to the drive home. With Richard and Olivia reluctantly squeezed in the back amongst the fold-back speakers and lighting stands, very tired and heartily sick of hearing the old man's band, we set off through the Dorset countryside.

June 12th

I take no chances this morning and head straight for the Paracetamol. No volleyball this afternoon, so time to recover.

A post-script to last night: Mum's youngest sister Denise and her husband Dick are spending the week-end down at Bournemouth. Opening yesterday evening's local paper, Dick, in his droll Lutonian drawl exclaims: "Gawd blimey! Thought I'd come down 'ere for a rest! You look through the local paper, hoping to find something different! What do you get? Sgt Pepper's Bleedin' Dart Board Band. Is there no getting away from your family?"

Actually, I think they were rather impressed, especially as we appeared to be playing in such a salubrious sounding place as the Central Hotel. Fortunately, their inability to attend insured our reputation for playing "classy do's" remained intact.

June 13th

The Bell, Walcot Street, Bath: It is the last day of the Bath Fringe Festival. Walcot Nation Day involves a street fair celebrating the Parish's "independence from the city of Bath" or some such historical anomaly. The street is closed off from traffic and stalls and stages are being set up. Pram race competitors assemble, jugglers, musicians and acrobats practise their stuff in anticipation of the one o'clock start and an enterprising Rastafarian sits on his doorstep under a sign that reads: "Jamaican jerky chicken and peas". We arrive early for this lunchtime performance and unload. The cars must be parked outside Walcot Street and this means driving around the residential roads of nearby Larkhall hoping to find a parking space. Cars in this neighbourhood are parked on inclines so steep as to appear almost vertical.

Back at The Bell we soundcheck. True to my word, I leave the Hofner behind and try out the white Washburn semi-acoustic guitar. It sounds and handles exquisitely. I feel almost confident enough to be audible. John is a veteran of The Bell. He explains how the positioning of the stage means the audience is in your face the whole time. It is also traditionally a serious music pub with a knowledgeable audience. The nerves are jangling louder than Taff's tambourine.

By one o'clock the pub is packed. Approximately two hundred or so squeeze in from the several thousands lining the streets outside. Perhaps another hundred or so listen from the pub's rear terrace. The first set warms them up nicely. John is on magnificent form having decided to play without the use of music sheets. This frees him up to join in with the banter. Rarely have we managed to sustain so many scripted and ad-libbed gags to such effect. The audience are clearly in holiday mood and John and I are bouncing off them and one another like a couple of trampolinists. The sound is well-balanced and in musician's parlance "as tight as a duck's arse." Lester and Taff on backing vocals are coming through clearly and Rob is swelling the sound with subtle assertiveness.

"I Am the Walrus", "Hello Goodbye" and "Hey Jude" seem to bring even more in off the street. The Bell is 'T' shaped with a short down-stroke. The stage is on the middle of the crosspiece with audience directly facing and looking on from both other sides. John is correct in his assertion... we appear confronted uncompromisingly from all angles. Even so, I manage to get in amongst them for the sing-a-long choruses. The room is stifling and it is especially hot under our heavy costumes. It is a sweaty, intense but effervescent atmosphere. Half way through "Get Back" John looks down and is delighted to see his two young lads Greg and Guy peering up at him having attended the fair with his ex-wife, Alison. This seems to provide an extra shot of adrenaline and the volume rises another notch. By now, the whole place is throbbing and all seats have been abandoned for a hard fought square foot on the floor, or in a couple of instances, the table tops.

Sunday newspaper headlines of "Kosovo Liberated" loom up from the tables and "All You Need is Love" resounds so loudly half of Bath could hear. "I Wanna Hold Your Hand" and "She Loves You" deliver greater delirium. "Twist and Shout" is almost drowned by the noise of audience participation. The resultant roar on the final chord is like lifting the F.A.Cup... and it goes on... and on. The windows shake with the screams of delight. We cannot even pretend to leave the stage before the encore. Lester's legs remain firmly crossed.

A lady in the audience proudly shows us the impressive water-colours she has sketched as we played. Another artist approaches us to pose for photo-montage he has in mind. A very attractive young blonde for reasons best known to herself, asks for a photograph with "George". Video cameras have been rolling throughout, calling cards are taken and new bookings suggested.

"We could be heroes" as Bowie would say. Backstage, we take off the wigs, the make-up and the coats and return to pack up, totally unmolested in a rapidly emptying bar. I go home, have a cup of tea and mark an exam paper or two.

June 16th

At one time the town of Street (which is technically classified as a village... the biggest in England) was almost entirely in the grip of the benevolent but zealous Clark family. Their shoe factory provided thousands of jobs in the Glastonbury area and this Quaker family saw to it that their workers were properly housed and reasonably paid. In return they developed a community in which the Quaker religion became solidly supported with the consequence that public houses were notable by their absence. Up until quite recent years, all hotels and the local Strode Theatre were forbidden licences to serve intoxicating liquor. Though the family still maintains the business; corporate investment, dependence on cheap labour abroad and the metamorphosis of the main factory into a shopping theme park (Clark's Village), have seen the traditions of this Somerset settlement seriously eroded.

Despite this, a "fun day out" is anticipated in July 2000 on the site of Street's other main employer and institution, Millfield. Thousands of workers (now mostly in administration) and their families are expected to attend and so Millfield's Development Manager, Douglas Humphrey has come to me with an interesting proposal.

Douglas is an ex-bomb squad officer. I cannot resist the temptation to occasionally assert that his shortfall in the thumbs and fingers department is down to nothing more than an altercation with a particularly stubborn Flymo. Nonetheless, he provides me with a fair bit of interesting holiday work and wants to get me "on board for this Clark's shindig." An outdoor concert has been proposed and Douglas is keen to promote Sgt Pepper. The Clark's people are reluctant to give up the idea of the Royal Philharmonic Orchestra but Douglas, who I would hardly classify as being "in tune with the proletariat" thinks they need something a bit more popular to precede the inevitable firework display. The money on offer is in line with some of the more impudent fees quoted by other, so-called "top" tribute bands. The trouble is that Douglas has an Abba fetish and wants me seek out some suitable doppelgangers to prop up the bill.

Given five years experience in directing the open air opening night of the Bath Festival, I'm fairly conversant with setting up these events but I find my reborn enthusiasm dampened by the possibility of having to play host to an overpaid Abba support act. Douglas, desperate to "get these Abba wallahs in the ranks" has received a demo video from an agency in Essex who still proudly boast representing Who Two despite having never made the effort to discover that we disbanded four years ago. The Abba tribute on the video will remain, for purposes of litigation, unnamed. Their act, caught in all its glory at a night club in Staines or somewhere, demonstrates slick professionalism in terms of costume changes and well-produced backing tracks but the performers exude all the personality of perfume reps in a department store. Also the girls seem a little miscast. The blonde one in Abba, as I recall, was, for all her cuteness, a bit on the lardy-arsed side. Here we see "the dark one" (I never could remember which was which) girded in a miniskirt which paradoxically reveals thighs that could crack nuts. The "blonde" tributee is the more svelte of the pseudo-Swedes, but in vain attempt to distract the audience from her partner's burgeoning buttocks, adorns a wig of glistening white nylon. The voices are good but whilst both singers concentrate on close harmonies in the choruses, the melody line seems to drop out as if Benny and Bjorn or possibly their backing tapes, aren't up to it.

Later, in Frome I bump into Marina Sossi, an ex-pupil and Drama graduate who appeared in *Waterloo Sunset*. Marina is in Planet Janet a send-up of a sixties style girlie trio along with Stuart's wife Claudia. I tell Marina about the video. I'm sure she could get a better (and cheaper) Abba tribute together if she wanted. She is highly amused by the video as described. Marina's diverse sense of humour soon comes up with the idea of having an entirely obese Abba tribute, wearing "fat suits" and going under the name Flabba. I somehow think this wasn't what Douglas had in mind.

June 18th

When we proudly announced from the stage at The Bell that our next gig was at the Civil Service Club, the audience hooted with derisive laughter. As we discover, the club is hardly the happening place in Bath Spa but the function draws in a sizeable audience.

Organised by Tom Sangster who is an ardent promoter and supporter, the event is to raise money for old people's accommodation. Well, you never know when you might be needing it do you? Tom has provided a backcloth to brighten up the performing area. At the top of the cloth are the words "Beatles Tribute" in a cardboard and crepe paper arrangement prompting Freeman's highly disrespectful onstage quip: "Thanks Tom, we've always dreamed of seeing our name up in cardboard."

June 19th - I'm So Tired:

Dickstock. Yes, Dickstock: A free festival on a farm somewhere in deepest Dorset. An old colleague at Frome College Clive Westmacott, has sensibly gone into farming. Every year he invites 500 or so to an evening of music. Commemorative T-shirts have been produced featuring the bands names as ingredients on a Marmite-style Dickstock jar. They make excellent souvenirs and pull in a few pounds for charity.

Dickstock is the one free charity gig a year we don't mind doing. Clive and Jo are well organised and the event is small enough to be friendly, but large enough to build a great atmosphere. One would also feel secure in the knowledge that Clive would deal with unwanted guests in much the same way as he dealt with unco-operative pupils in woodwork lessons. That is, by brandishing a piece of threatening two-by-four in hands so large that they should be classified licensed weapons. "Girt Shovel 'ands" the boys at school used to call him.

The stage is set in a Dutch barn. The open sides allow the audience to spread around the adjoining paddock but offer shelter against inclement weather. It's the ideal compromise for an English summer evening.

John has managed to negotiate Neon Monkey (our respective sons' band) onto the support bill. It is their first gig for several months, being too young for the usual pub circuit. It is hard to review their act objectively but, once again, I am astonished by their confidence and musicianship. Tom is a most charismatic front man. He sings with melodic conviction and his guitar work justifies the years of tuition. Learning to play properly was always the deal when Tom first decided he wanted a guitar. I was determined not to pass on my own inadequacies.

In a predominantly Green Day inspired set, the bass and drums have to be attacked with controlled vigour. Richard and Greg are a superb pairing. At thirteen, John's eldest is a precocious percussionist, demonstrating a fluency clearly born of Tony Stockley's expert tuition. Richard casually holds down solid but quite intricate bass lines and is now contributing important backing vocals. With Tom's mate Mark Dixon layering power chords over this tight rhythm section, Neon Monkey could quite easily be re-packaged as the next boy band. Pleasingly, they've got too much musical integrity for that to happen.

Following a high-energy band called Snide and with a huge bonfire blazing in the paddock, Sgt Pepper take the stage before an audience well warmed up. It is a ninety minute, non-stop, no holds-barred, finger-blistering blast. Marina and Claudia from Planet Janet are particularly complimentary about the look and sound of the new line-up.

Being John Lennon

Stuart, whose drumming engagements with the Janets some-times give us cause to re-call Tony Stockley, is rightly relish-ing the praise heaped upon him for taking over the Ringo songs. Unlike Ringo he manages to affect just the right tone and expression without exhibiting more flats than a Liver-pool Council Estate. Claudia and Stuart are expecting their first baby in a couple of weeks and so our youngest member is set to take July off. I bet Stockley's brushing up on his "Yellow Submarine" as I write.

Overnight camping at Dickstock seemed a good idea at the time. Neon Monkey's Mark has persuaded his mum Alison and partner Brian to bring the caravan and (in cel-ebration of the boy's sixteenth birthday) provide a barbecue. They are ardent supporters of Sgt Pepper and so the pre-show party is soon dominated by a bunch of middle-aged freeloading musicians who can spot a complimentary scoff when they see one.

At 2 a.m. Anne and I decide to retire for the night. A tangerine VW Beetle containing four 20-year olds suddenly draws alongside our tents. With headlights turning every camper in the vicinity into an unwitting silhouette and the car stereo pumping techno beats so loudly that the Beetle seems about to shed its shell, Anne politely requests the occu-pants be less intrusive on behalf of the children in the party. Their compliant departure from our spot is marred by the driver's intoxication, resulting in the accidental extinguish-ing of aforementioned headlights and the need for guidance as to the purpose of a steering wheel.

Having tried in vain to coax Olivia to sleep and failed to persuade Richard not to abandon his own tent for our already overcrowded accommodation, I eventually slip under the quilt which serves as a substitute for the sleeping bag stolen earlier that evening.

My head, reeling from less sleep than the average junior

doctor, lays finally upon the soft pillow when the unmistakable, throat-clearing staccatto of a Volkswagen Beetle rumbles alongside us. The continual thudding of this mobile disco threatens to outwardly propel the vehicle's windows and decapitate several sheep in nearby fields. I look out of the tent and flash a torch at the car. Others camping around us are forcibly expressing their preference not to sleep in the full glare of the headlights. "For fuck's sake turn it down," I yell, much to my kids' embarrassment. Again the car draws away and we hold our breath in the hope that the driver successfully slaloms through the tents.

Half an hour of tossing and turning later, my eyelids begin to draw heavily down when, true to form, the evil Beetle scuttles back to its favourite patch. I hold my breath for a minute or so, hoping without real expectation that the occupants might consider the possibility of a) turning off the engine; b) switching off the lights and c) reducing the noise from the car stereo to something remotely resembling the more restrained levels of a rave party. I finally and inevitably snap. Unzipping the tent as if skinning a wildebeest, I storm out into the pitch night, barefoot across the long, rain-drenched grass, wearing nothing but a pair of pastel-blue pants. Wrenching open the passenger-side door, I yell with enough force to wake several surrounding villages, "Are you taking the fucking piss? You've been asked three times to shut up! Now turn off the fucking stereo, put out the fucking lights; switch off the fucking engine or fuck off somewhere else!" I may have said "fuck" at least once more but I have no idea how it might have scanned into this scatological outpouring.

Strangely, it seemed to do the trick. No more was heard from our tangerine, insect-encrusted ensemble. Peace of mind however, was not the outcome of this act of verbal barbarity. With heart and adrenaline pumping away towards the dawn, I lay awake awaiting the first signs of reprisal. "Any moment now," I thought, "any moment now that tent is going to come flapping down around our ears." Or worse still, I imagined being found embedded in the field with mysterious tyre tracks imprinted on my exposed torso; the local paper headlines pronouncing: "Beetle crushes Beatle in Festival Field Fury."

June 20th

Desperate for a proper night's sleep, I manage to stay awake until 10 p.m. when our German exchange student is due to arrive. Rob and I patrol the Frome College car park pondering what we'd let our respective families in for, when Mike Walker arrives in haste to apologise to the assembled parents. "They're running late. Currently on the M4 at Reading. Should be with us in an hour." Mike's approximation explains why he has previously served a ban for driving with excessive speed. Reading is a good ninety minutes away. The choice of the M4 rather than the M3 suggests further delays are in store.

Two hours later the German and Czech company arrive, led by the formidable Christine Beutelhoff. Christine is partially sighted but this would not have deterred her from giving directions to the coach driver. This cultural partnership began eleven years ago when Christine was unable to secure a drama exchange with Homberg's twin town of Bridgwater. Now Bridgwater might more appropriately be twinned with Chernobyl, so this was no great setback. She was subsequently recommended to approach friendly old Frome. Christine wrote to me explaining that she produced plays in English and was keen to bring them to England in return for us performing in Germany. At the time I couldn't imagine compromising my family life any further for my "art". I politely wrote back suggesting that I was busy and maybe next year we could consider hosting them. Before I knew it, a small platoon of Germans had formed a bridge-head at Bath railway station in the final push for the Frome frontier.

The following year Frome College revived *Terms of Engagement* my play about the Falklands conflict to a highly tolerant and appreciative audience in Homberg. The first problem was deciding which of a number of variations of the name Homberg we were headed for. Fortunately we alighted at the right one, a small town south of Kassel in central Germany. Homberg happens to have the most exquisitely Germanic town square and yet is of no apparent consequence to the German tourist industry. I immediately fell in love with Homberg. Anne and I have made many friends there in our subsequent visits.

Mike Walker has moved the exchange on by incorporating the Anglo-Czech School from Ceske Budejovice in a three-way partnership. Budejovice or Budweis is the home of Budvar beer, the far superior inspiration for Budweiser. Budejovice was a major stop on our *All You Need is Love* tour. It has a magnificently ornate Bohemian town centre and the local beer is about ten times cheaper than in England. It is the greatest place in the world to get drunk.

After greeting Christine, who was already making one of her customary speeches to the assembled throng almost as soon as the coach door hissed open, I swiftly welcomed her delightful colleague Luise and their Czech counterpart Katarine. Rapidly, I sought out our exchange student Nicole and the poor girl was whisked off into the English night by a man she had never met, to an unknown destination. When I explained that I had a wife and three children she looked understandably relieved. After a rapid tour of bath-room facilities, she gratefully took to the highly make-shift bed in the rapidly converted study, looking every bit as tired as myself.

Being John Lennon

June 22nd

Anne and I meet the indomitable Christine and friends in the Farmer's Arms. Within a few minutes of re-acquainting, Christine has moved the subject of conversation on to the next exchange. Christine is a great one for planning ahead. She has an energy and determination which are admirable and quite exhausting.

Like her husband Ludwig, who is completely blind, Christine adapts admirably to the demands of everyday life. Ludwig went blind as the result of a faulty vaccine administered as a child in an American military hospital when suffering scarlet fever during the post-war occupation years. Ludwig is a brilliant chess player and able to describe journeys, routes and distances with far greater exactitude than a sighted person.

When staying with her on my first visit to Homberg, one particular incident exemplified how the blind must adjust to a daily routine in which the mundane can become farcical: Christine and I arrived on her doorstep after a night at the local bierkeller. Finding the keyhole required of Christine, a great deal of determination as she bent almost double with her better eye homing in on the lock like a hunter staring in the sights of a rifle. The door finally open, she switches on the hall light and there, a matter of two feet away stands Ludwig, suddenly illuminated. I nearly jump backwards onto the doorstep. "Good evening," says Ludwig in the slow, deliberate tone of a Gothic manservant. I am half expecting him to say, "The master has been expecting you." My instinctive reaction is to wonder why the bloody hell he is walking around with the lights off. Then I remember.

Christine has proved a brilliant tour manager for our productions, despite them being performed in English. I am delighted when, without prompting, Christine invites the

Dart Board Band to Germany in the summer of next year. Katerine immediately responds with the offer of a performance in Budejovice. She believes she can also fix us up with other notable venues. Luise chips in with some suggestions as to how we might extend the tour to southern Germany and by the end of the evening we're talking about an impressive two-week schedule of castles, houseboats and halls. Families will be welcomed and accommodated. Christine can be pushy and unremitting – but by God, she's reliable. If Christine says the tour will happen, then no other guarantee is necessary. All I have to do now is persuade the band and more importantly, their wives of this very exciting proposition.

June 24th

The Homberg and Czech group presents their play *Amusing Yourself to Death* at The Merlin. It's a company-devised show with an environmental theme. As ever, the English is excellent and the movement and dance beautifully executed. The educational value is self-evident.

The big news of the day is that HTV want the Dart Board Band to do a studio recording in late July for their Friday evening show *The Pleasure Guide*. This will be a plug for our performance the next day at The Rondo Theatre, Bath, which is already selling well.

My enthusiasm is tempered though by a similar recording of Who Two during which the presenter did his best to make us look a bunch of geriatric amateurs sadly addicted to re-living their youth. This time the wig stays firmly on.

June 25th - 8.00 pm

I drop Tom and Mark Dixon off at Pilton. It is the boy's first Glastonbury Festival without me. Rites of passage for today's teenager seem to include Glastonbury high up the list, along with the first beer, snog, fag and shag.

I am pleasantly surprised to have beaten the festival traffic on my way to work and look on the Worthy Farm site with mixed feelings. Part of me thinks it is the most over-rated, over-grown, filthy and decadent event on earth. The other part wants to be in there, preferably on the stage, soaking up the atmosphere. Though one of the worst experiences of my life as a performer, I have attained so much kudos from unknowing acquaintances for having played Glastonbury, that I feel highly tempted to give it another go. Next time however, there will be no subtle dialogue or cleverly integrated songs. Next time it'll be a brash, unpretentious Beatles bash, preferably supported by a 50 kilowatt sound system. I vow to get in touch with organisers Michael Eavis and Arabella Churchill about next year. Despite having very positive dealings with both in the past I am by no means confident they'll find us the appropriate platform. If successful however, our itinerary for the summer of next year will be packed with outdoor concerts which will hopefully play a significant part in raising our profile.

9.00 pm

The first of two successive performances at Shillingstone. Terry, the landlord, has clearly over-estimated our popularity in what is, after all, a village pub. Although all one hundred tickets are sold for tomorrow, we find no "spin off" trade and struggle tonight to make twenty. Anne, having accompanied our German guests on a pleasure boat cruise to Bath, arrives late along with Nicole and two other Homberg students. They have been delayed by a cock-up on the arrangements front with communications between Mike and Christine finally reaching a complete breakdown. Both have highly assertive and conflicting personalities. It is a minor miracle that neither of them ended the "pleasure cruise" being dredged from the Avon by a Police Diving Team.

June 26th

I say my farewells to the delightful Nicole before heading off for Shillingstone. Despite our fears about welcoming a sixteen-year-old girl into a house dominated by two teen-age boys, Nicole has been the most co-operative and charming of guests. Tom and Richard, acutely embarrassed by the prospect of sharing so much as a meal, not to mention a bathroom with our attractive visitor, have both kept a safe distance. I write farewell cards for Anne to pass on to Christine and co. The band has really warmed to the idea of going back into Europe, this time as a self-contained act in our own right.

"You only play Shillingstone twice. Once on the way up and once on the way down." Those in the audience who have returned for second helpings get the joke straight away. This time they are joined by a coach party from Poole who are determined to enjoy the evening at all costs. Familiar faces also appear from gigs played elsewhere. It is genuinely humbling when people are prepared to go out of their way to attend our performances.

The only blemish on the evening was the late arrival of two clearly underage and over imbibed youths. Stumbling towards the stage, they attempt to dance but have no discernible control over their legs. As they lurch across the room, one boy clatters the lighting stand which threatens to topple over, concussing, burning or electrocuting those close by. The other boy meanwhile, is making a habit of lurching into my microphone stand, causing the mic to hammer loudly against my front teeth. Out of the context of a school room, I find I have little patience with unruly youths. I go from being Mr. Chips to Victor Meldrew in an instant. I see John wince as I project my boot firmly up aforementioned youth's arse with the accompanying invitation (off-mic) to "fuck off". Of course, as an inveterate coward I am aware that our

mate Colin, a burly copper, whose wedding to Judy we "offi-
ciated" last year, is standing between the lads and ourselves.
They apologise and eventually slope off. What with this and
the Dickstock Beetle incident, I'll soon be labelled "the hard
man of the Dorset county rock scene." Hmmmmn...

The coach party from Poole are decidedly happy and will
recommend us most highly to the local branch of the Conservative Club. I think they enjoyed the arse-kicking incident most of all.

June 27th

All the mobile phone networks at Pilton are jammed so we
have heard nothing from my son Tom in the last two days.
This confirms my belief that technology causes greater stress
than it relieves. I head off for the festival site in the hope
he will be waiting to be picked up. As I crawl in the traffic
jam full of Sunday afternoon gatecrashers, I catch site of
him looking more tanned and blonde than when he left.
This year the weather has been almost perfect. He looks so
tall and adult standing there wearing new, rather trendy sunglasses that I have to look twice to ensure it is him. He clambers aboard looking relieved to see me. He is at that age
when communication can be very difficult. He would never
actually admit he's happy to see me but I pick up the subtle
messages.

Tom has his final GCSE exam in Drama tomorrow afternoon. We're very much counting on this as one of his better
subjects, so I insist he has to miss out on the last day the
festival to ensure a decent night's sleep. His feet are aching
and highly blistered from wearing new boots over the weekend. He is distinctly crusty and unless I'm very much mistaken, probably in need of more than just a good shower. He
recounts the inevitable horror story of Glastonbury toilets.
His utter distaste at the sanitation is put into perspective
when I regale him with the familiar legend of the collaps-

ing Glastonbury toilet block which, one year, hurled the occupants into the lime pit below and resulted in a helicopter winching them from a sea human excrement. A bit like being rescued off the coast of Blackpool I would imagine.

Despite every indication of being glad to be home, by the evening Tom has come to realise that all his friends are enjoying (I use the word in its broadest sense) Skunk Anansie, while he is curled up revising from a battered copy of *Our Day Out* by Willie Russell. For me that summarises the real pulling power of The Glastonbury Festival. It is a massive exercise in self-delusion and peer-group pressure. If that mystical Tor really does emanate some kind of cosmic influence, its vibes probably transmit the following:

"No matter what your discomfort; no matter what poverty you endure; no matter how you arrive; no matter how you enter; no matter that Tony Bennett is topping the bill... get thee to Glastonbury. For there will you surely not be left out."

Must... try... to get... on the Healing Field stage... next... year...

June 29th

Phil Moakes, erstwhile sound-man and now unlikely but effective Town Councillor phones. In his new found office he has been nominated to serve on the Cheese and Grain Hall sub-committee. He has been going through the accounts and wants to double-check our receipts from the February appearance. Strangely enough, our figures and the hall's do not match. Something is amiss. He voices serious concerns about the manager's determination not to go to contract with any acts that perform there.

Last week, when trying her now customary last-minute re-think on an "arrangement" she claims the artist engaged resolved their differences by picking up the entire revenue from the box-office table and walking out. She has now demanded yet another month off with work-related stress. Something is rotten in The Cheesey Groin.

The Idiot's Guide... No: 6
I Saw Her Standing There

A prime example of the Dart Board Band taking liberties: The first song on the first Beatles album. It swings along in a nice, inoffensive James Last sort of way. McCartney's doing a bit of a Pat Boone on vocals.

Several years later, post-Beatles, John Lennon makes an unexpected appearance at Madison Square Garden in front of 20,000 ecstatic Americans and one estranged Japanese wife.

This performance reunites Lennon with Yoko Ono, proving that as much as some people seek to be control freaks, there are others only too willing to let them.

Lennon has teamed up with Elton John and is about to terminate his brief appearance "so I can get can out of here and be sick" with a song written by "an old estranged fiancé of mine called Paul." It is an evening for reunions. Elton John's line-up launch into a Chuck Berry riff with all the subtlety of a newly formed garage band, while John and Elton pitch in with a frenetic "She was just seventeen..." This is the version Sgt Pepper's Only Dart Board Band find easiest to copy as, in this instance, we suffer less by comparison.

Actually, I love the Lennon and Elton John version because of its spontaneity and vigour. In short, *it rocks*. We originally included "I Saw Her Standing There" as a barely rehearsed jam and it worked. We then added a few refinements like singing the second middle eight accompanied only by a drum beat and hand clapping, shoving in a guitar solo for Lester and giving Rob a well-earned piano solo. I sing Lennon style and John adds a harmony throughout verses two and three. The song builds nicely and by restraining slightly from an all out heavy rock interpretation, it gains momentum and keeps the punters on their toes. The Beatles it ain't. But no one's complained yet.

Another example of how a song can develop in rehearsal is the jaunty "I Should Have Known Better". The Beatles in performance sometimes missed out harmonica solos because Lennon hadn't perfected the art of singing and playing mouth harp at the same time. This involves considerable buttock dexterity which John was naturally reluctant to demonstrate in the company of Brian Epstein. I miss out the harmonica bits mainly because I can't play it. Instead Rob cheats them in with a very authentic keyboard sound.

Everything else on "I Should Have Known Better" goes as on the record except the vocals. In rehearsals, having first listened to the original, we played through the song with me singing the melody line and John singing the harmony below. We then played through the CD again to discover a significant mistake. There is no harmony. It's just a John Lennon vocal double-tracked to thicken the sound. The thing was, the harmony sounded good. Infact, dare I say it, it sounded better? I am convinced that, in some of the early recordings, limited studio time meant records were released in a more simple, undeveloped form than George Martin might have wished.

Anyway, either audiences don't notice the changes we make or don't care. It would probably take the most ardent, anorak-wearing Beatles musicologist to notice all the subtle changes but it doesn't stop us from continually debating the quality of our playing and the level to which we should aspire to complete authenticity. Personally I do not believe in a slave-like devotion to original recordings. It was noticed by one knowledgable spectator that a well-known Beatles tribute, "sound exactly like the CD." He continued, "Trouble is, I don't want to go to the theatre to listen to a CD." My sentiments entirely. Furthermore, had The Beatles continued to play live, McCartney's own shows with Wings and Lennon's brief appearance with Elton John suggest that they too would have adapted the material freely.

Is the above a justification or an excuse? Who cares? Back to the diary...

July

July 3rd

Parents Day at Millfield. A casual stroll around the grounds watching the cricket, the tennis and the celebrity parents. Actually, *Hello* magazine wouldn't have given much space to this year's turn out... no James Bonds or the like loitering around the toilets for a quick fag. After a pleasant buffet lunch, I beat a hasty retreat to begin nine weeks summer holiday. Yes, isn't life a bitch?

With no Holiday Village at Millfield this year, my workaholic tendencies will only be satisfied by band work. Arriving home, I have about one hour in which to change clothes and pack the car so as to reach Clearwell Castle in time to set up for tonight's wedding reception.

The others have paired up on transport but my car is too full for passengers. I would have welcomed not driving today in order to enjoy one of the most scenic routes we are likely to undertake.

Crossing the old Severn Bridge, we turn north to Chepstow. A short delay occurs owing to heavy traffic leaving the racecourse. I had no idea there was such a demand for bourgeois entertainment in South Wales. Taking the Monmouth road, we follow the Wye Valley through Tintern, past the Abbey ruin. Having never taken this route before, I am hugely distracted by its beauty. Tintern village reminds me of a coastal fishing port in Cornwall. The River Wye expands on a wide curve creating an unsullied beach at low tide. Tea shops, hotels and quaint houses line the front below a steep bank of cliffs. The road weaves through lush forest and hillside. Traffic signs warn of badgers in the vicinity as if travelling through a wildlife park. We cross over a small bridge over the Wye back into England and follow a narrow road up to Clearwell Castle on the edge of the Forest of Dean in Gloucestershire.

The castle is Gothic revival, early eighteenth century or so I am informed by Rob, who is a surveyor in real life. It was used as a residential recording studio by Led Zeppelin. Having survived that particular onslaught, it is now a popular venue for weddings and receptions but is otherwise closed to the public.

Roger has booked us to play at his daughter's wedding. He is a pub owner. One of his assets was the King's Arms in one of the less salubrious back streets of Bath, where we played many of our early gigs. If you knew the King's Arms you'd realise that this was not the place for Roger to impress his new, wealthy in-laws from Colorado.

The castle's architects made few concessions to whatever the equivalent of a rock band was in 1730. The function room is a reasonable size but the main access leads straight through the middle of the stage area. Given that there is a support band and we are both expected to set up on the same stage whilst allowing a central corridor for guests to pass through; ingenuity and co-operation are the order of the day. The support band is called Souled Out. Their set of soul covers is very impressive and fortunately contrasts nicely with our own act. The musicianship and presentation are highly professional and it is no surprise to discover that they are in great demand. In the long wait before the action starts we swap anecdotes and contacts. If they have any objection to preceding us on the bill, they don't show it. Both bands are very relaxed. There is no sense of rivalry that sometimes occurs when bands lack genuine confidence in their ability. With Who Two, despite developing a powerful act, we were sometimes taken aback by being top of the bill, perhaps underestimating our own qualities. We would sit through the first act desperately hoping they wouldn't upstage us. Daft really. Nobody ever upstaged The Who and we weren't a bad substitute... so to speak.

Souled Out play on an unhelpful diagonal to the audience but still get them up dancing. They predictably over-run and are slow getting out. We re-configure our equipment hastily but John is unhappy with the sound balance and Roger starts getting shirty about sound-checks, demanding we "just get on with it." We are more conscious than ever of giving a good account of ourselves and with myself harbouring a sore throat, we begin the set with a sense of trepidation.

Putting down the guitar and using an extended mic cable to get out into the audience and encourage a lot of community singing, enables me to hear the band from the audience's perspective. Despite all our reservations, my throat holds out, the balance is good and the audience very appreciative. Our confidence grows throughout the 90-minute "straight through" set which extends to two hours after insistent demands for encores. Roger makes amends with a little cash bonus at the end of the evening.

The journey back through the dark country roads is less of a pleasure. Tintern Abbey looks distinctly haunted and a sense of foreboding follows me for several miles on the approach to Bath in the shape of a police car with little else to do at 2.30 on a Sunday morning. The only way I could tell it was a police car was due to the fact that no other driver in his right mind would drive right up the rear of another vehicle at forty miles an hour with a clear road ahead. They almost demand you break the speed limit just to give them something to do.

As he finally speeds by, I thank my good fortune in replacing the dodgy brake light before leaving home. Rock'n'roll drinking excesses are sadly out of the question for the jobbing musician whose driving licence is almost as much a part of his livelihood as is his instrument.

July 9th

Another stately home. The West Country owes much of its historic buildings to the tobacco and slavery barons of Bristol. Kingweston House is one such monument, now in the ownership of Millfield as a boarding house. The mansion grounds also provide the school with its main football pitches. Five miles from the school itself, Kingweston can be a pleasant retreat from the Millfield campus, unless you happen to be refereeing a fourth team fixture on a wet Saturday in January, with a numbing South Westerly blowing across the high, flat, plain.

On this still, July evening, Kingweston hosts a charity ball in a huge marquee. This event is being run by Ian Hunt, an international basketball player and coach and Fiona and Richard Ellison; Richard being the former England and Kent cricketer. Both Ian and Richard teach at Millfield and serve as constant reminders as to the irony of the school expecting the likes of me to coach football.

The ball is attended by a large number of Millfield staff but fortunately has a wider appeal so as not to resemble a school function. With term well and truly finished, it is a great (if expensive) opportunity to unwind. Not for me though. Naturally I have snapped up the chance to pitch Sgt Pepper as the evening's cabaret for the second year running.

The fee is dropped considerably as the event is a fundraiser for cancer charities, though we are aware that the DJ is probably getting more than the rest of us combined.

Being John Lennon

Tonight's DJ by chance, is Andrew Carpenter, Frome's very own "Mr Entertainment". No issue of the *Somerset Standard* would be complete without a photo of Andrew smiling through innumerable teeth like a game show host, as he promotes his latest disco/ pantomime/ musical appearance/ promotion/ new car. (Delete as applicable). In the past I have often snootily looked on Andrew as my light entertainment alter-ego. We were born within a few weeks of one another and conform to the absurdly ambitious Sagittarian stereotype; juggling careers, interests and families in a vain attempt at self-glorification. (Not that I believe in all that superstitious stuff, you understand). While I was engaged in aesthetic pursuits and trying to "push back the boundaries" of dramatic art, Andrew was cultivating his persona as the nightclub king of the West. Now here we are sharing the limelight in an evening of unpretentious hedonistic pleasure. My, haven't I come a long way?

Andrew has recently re-invented his stage personality in the form of Johnny Inferno, an afro-wigged, handle-bar moustachioed seventies throwback in white flares and butterfly collars. This is frightening. At forty-two we both seem to be re-constructing our youth through our public performances and finding devious ways of hiding our tell-tale receding hairlines.

Before we go on, I break the good news that Taff and Claudia have had a girl, last night. Rob responds: "Well, he could have done the gig after all. I played the night our Ben was born." We look on in disbelief knowing that Rob's wife Tonya, like most of our partners, is not always happy at playing the rock widow. "Well, caesarean, wasn't it? Nothing I could do. Had to let Tonya get on with it." In our minds, Tonya suddenly takes on a saintly virtue.

After the auction, in which Pierce Brosnan's James Bond dinner suit went for over eight hundred quid, we begin to a fairly muted reception. I assume this is because most people know us by now. To my surprise however, one or two familiar faces are clearly bewildered when I address them from the stage in the Scouse accent. They try to get a closer look, squinting and smiling benignly as if trying to X-ray through the hair, glasses and moustache.

Well plastered by the time we begin, people quickly get onto the floor and we juggle the set around to keep them dancing. A bunch of guys are wearing kilts which, I suspect, has less to do with heritage than granting them easy access should they end the night shagging behind a nearby tree. In true Celtic tradition, these well-spoken Camerons, Findlays and Campbells are struggling to maintain control over their over-exposed lower bodies. Halfway through "Hey Bulldog" one such McTavish trips over his own feet and hurtles headlong into our speaker stand starting a domino effect of disco speakers and amplifiers heading simultaneously in a easterly direction. Andrew attempts to intercept the collapsing columns only to sustain a broken finger for his troubles. McTavish meanwhile, is sprawling across the front of the low stage rostra in pool of alcohol, glass and vomit whilst others of the clan look on laughing. I hurriedly try to re-set the speaker on top of the aluminum stand but it has buckled and bent beyond the ability to stay upright. Holding the heavy speaker aloft, I find myself being tickled under the arms by a shamelessly drunk young female telling me not to be cross. I plead with her forcibly to stop but she accuses me of being an "old misery", before I finally dump the cabinet on the floor perilously close to (but sadly not upon) her delicately painted toenails.

As "Bulldog" ends I remark that: "I used to be in a Who tribute band but we never managed to smash up our gear quite so badly as that." What is going through my mind is the sizeable cheque I had just handed over to pay-off Mike for the PA the night before. "I wouldn't mind," I add, "but he's only 'ad a couple of shandies." It has become clearly apparent that I am in a strop and cannot hide my genuine contempt for this act of desecration. It then occurs to me that while I am berating sections of the audience, I am doing so as John Lennon, not as myself. The accent has become an innate part of my onstage personality. I couldn't shake it off when doing the recent solo spots in school concerts either. What is happening to me? Why am I speaking like this? Why do I seem to be so confrontational onstage? I decide to go home and talk it over with Yoko.

July 10th

The Black Swan, Trowbridge. New tenants, new decor. Same old customers. Overheard at bar before gig:

RUBY: *(Middle aged, Tarty, Out to pull.)* "Christ! I'm fuckin' swelterin'."

EDNA: *(Middle aged, overweight with an accent combining the burr of Long John Silver and the gravelly depth of Frank Bruno).* "Fuckin' 'ell! Innit fuckin' 'ot in 'ere?"

RUBY: Too fuckin' 'ot to pull tonight, Edna.

EDNA: You know what I'm gonna 'ave to fuckin' do to cool off?

RUBY: Oh, fer fuck's sake! Don't get your fuckin' tits out again! Not in 'ere!

EDNA: No. Don't be fuckin' daft! I wouldn't do that. Not in 'ere. I was gonna take me cacks off. I ain't changed 'em fer a couple days. Stink like fuck! I was gonna wave 'em round make a bit of space.

RUBY: That'll soon clear the fuckin' room!

Deciding a conversation on the works of Renee Descartes was out of the question, I move on to the music organiser at the Swan, Alan Sad. Yes, Alan Sad. I am not making this up. Alan is talking with his almost identical brother, Ken Sad. I once called Alan "a sad case" for coming to so many of our gigs. I had no idea of his name at the time and spent weeks trying to figure out why he looked like he was going to punch me in the face. Alan Sad and Ken Sad look like slightly reformed Hell's Angels, all leather waistcoats and handlebar moustaches... except Alan, who has shaved his off. I use the clean-shaven look as an excuse for not giving him Mike's role as Bingo. Alan loves Bingo and is distraught not to be hearing his bulldog impersonations again.

ALAN: Where is he then? Where's old Bingo?

ME: He left a few weeks ago.

ALAN: Why's that then?

ME: Hip replacement.

ALAN: No!

ME: Yeah. Got back late after a gig and was locked out of the old people's home. So he tries shinning up the drain-pipe... it breaks. Broke his hip.

ALAN: (*Pause*) No, go on... why's he left?

ME: Well... (*Long, boring explanation*).

ALAN: I used to like 'im. It looked good with the three of you... up front like.

ME: He'll be pleased. I'll tell him next time I visit him in the home. So... wanna do the barking on "Bulldog" tonight, Alan?

ALAN: Fuck off! I'll be in the garden. Too bloody hot in here!

Fortunately, John has managed to persuade Tony to bring his equipment tonight as he was playing his "Ton-Up" Freeman role for Frome Cricket Club in Bristol. Ten minutes before the gig we are all set up, ready to go, but no sign of John. The pub phone rings. John has broken down outside Bath. Fortune smiles on him again in the form of an AA man who happens to be repairing a car within his view. Rob collects John while the AA man gets to work and we go up in a rush twenty minutes late. A reminder of New Years Eve and Lester's delay at Cardiff Airport comes to mind. Lester recently discovered that he would be returning from holiday in France the day of our first gig in September at Poole. When I asked if he was sure we should take the booking he replies with disarmingly casual confidence: "Of course. What could possibly go wrong?" I consider taking a crash course in playing lead guitar during the summer.

1.30 a.m. Enter Sandman... (Being the Metallica song of that title.)

I return home for an hour before driving a round trip of about ninety minutes to collect Tom and his mate from Bristol. They have taken a coach trip to see Metallica at Milton Keynes Bowl. Of course, being sixteen they made no consideration of how the hell they would get the remaining twenty-five miles from Bristol to Frome at 3.30 in the morning.

I leave in pitch darkness, sharing the road with only nocturnal wildlife and the criminally insane. After a maniac has nearly forced me into a ditch, a deer then delicately bounds before the car just outside Bath. I proceed with extreme caution from there on until picking up speed in central Bristol where it doesn't pay to remain stationary at 3.30 in the morning; unless of course, you are on the game. The coach, to my relief, gets in on time. The boys have enjoyed the day although it was slightly marred when Marilyn Manson, the absurdly androgynous support act to Metallica, was hit in the face onstage by a flying bottle. So... heavy metal fans are discerning after all.

I arrive home as dawn breaks and consider the possibility of a paper round.

July 15th

Visit opticians. Reading glasses recommended. Choose Lennon style, against Anne's better judgement.

Go to wig supplier and hairdresser Peggy Snook for wig

teasing session prior to week-end gigs and TV recording. Always willing to please, Peggy performs an even more radical haircut at my request as part of the service which, when coupled with new reading glasses, may enable me to increase my roster of characters to Alf Garnett and Dr Crippen.

July 16th - Getting Better All the Time:

The Woolley Festival is a promising new open-air weekend event, just outside Bradford on Avon. Being legendary in B on A, we are to headline the first night. On arriving, I wake up to the fact that this really is no mean achievement. The event looks extremely well organised with an enormous marquee all set to contain six or seven hundred standing punters, attracted by a varied programme from four bands.

As the Thin Ice Jazz Band kick the evening off, in the beer tent we are introduced to Nicky Byrne. He turns out to be a slight, very dapper gent of mature years who just happened to run The Beatles merchandising operation in the mid-sixties. At first we are a bit sceptical about the old boy's credentials, but it didn't take him long to convince us that, unlike much of The Beatles old merchandise, he was the genuine article. Nicky justifiably lays claim to engineering that mass hysteria at Kennedy Airport when the Fabs first arrived in the States. Apparently he offered a free T-shirt and a dollar to every kid who turned up on the day, thus creating probably the biggest truancy figures in New York's history.

Nicky seems in his element, as we gather round him like he is some kind of West Wilts Maharishi, listening to the improbable anecdotes. I couldn't help thinking of Jimmy the Lips in *The Commitments* with his endless bullshit stories of Elvis and the like. I write this having dipped into Philip Norman's book *Shout* only to find to my humility that Nicky was indeed "the real deal." It was Nicky's real deal with Brian Epstein however that was to be his undoing.

"Epstein was a complete fool. He had no idea about the business," says Nicky.

Whether taking advantage of this when negotiating 90% of Beatles merchandising profits to his own company, he didn't say. Needless to say it all ended in acrimony.

"Do you know what I got out of it?" this distinguished old toff says with a look of genuine sorrow in his eyes. "After all the litigation and legal costs? Ten thousand pounds. Now I live in a council flat in Trowbridge. But we're happy, aren't we darling?" he concludes, looking to his partner.

She smiles in sincere agreement. She is an artist, much younger than him, but probably a great deal more genuine than all the women he encountered in the sixties Chelsea set.

A tongue in cheek-rockabilly set from Bill Smarme and the Business was followed by a tribute to Santana, predictably called Sultana. The musicianship throughout is pretty bloody stunning and as John rightly points out we're going to have to go into "full show-biz personality overdrive" to justify our top billing.

With no soundcheck, but a reassuringly professional sound and lighting rig at our disposal, the stage is rapidly reset prior to our ten o'clock appearance. With Nicky's parable of The Beatles unimpressive Parisian encounter ringing in our ears, the adrenaline is pumping hard. The marquee is now solidly packed from end to end. An eccentric Master of Ceremonies with the verbal demeanor of Donald Sinden and a look that crosses a reformed Hell's Angel with an Italian tenor, introduces Nicky Byrne to the stage. Nicky says a few nice things about us, despite never having seen the act and sensibly doesn't attempt to spin them a yarn or two. The gregarious announcer spares us no blushes by introducing us as, "The greatest tribute band in the world." (I presume he meant West Wiltshire.) Rob enters, unassumingly playing our vaudeville-type vamp opening to "Penny Lane". Taff, having persuaded Claudia to give him the night off from changing the baby, picks up the beat; Lester follows on, strumming the chords as he enters and finally, John and I hit the front with a few quips, Music Hall style, whilst quickly slipping on guitars and leading off into the first verse. Naturally enough, my guitar amp is neither switched on nor miked up to the house sound system, but the sound man quickly leaps on the stage to make amends. Of course nobody in the audience would have noticed this in the least.

As we strike up "I Feel Fine", I brace myself for what is shaping up to be a show with more high octane energy than a Harrier jet fly-past. There is a high sense of expectation in the air. Since the Bath Fringe performance at The Bell, we keep hearing about ourselves in revered tones. Having learned my lesson from hyping Who Two only to be presented as a bunch of sad, middle-aged amateurs, the Peppers have done little to attract the local media, beyond gently plugging the odd gig. Nobody has ever been invited to review Sgt Pepper's Only Dart Board Band but tonight photos and reviews are promised in Monday's *Western Daily Press*. In addition, the Media Studies camera crew from the local college running around backstage in "exclusive" footage mode, helps give the Woolley Festival the atmosphere of a true "happening".

The onstage telepathy is working a dream. The audience begins to rock and sing early on but we manage to keep something in reserve. Songs like "Ticket to Ride" are easy enough to pull off convincingly but "A Day in the Life" proves to be the moment when we sense that we've completely won them over. With the guitar put to one side, my vocal is lifted by some spontaneous reverb courtesy of the sound engineer, giving the same eerie, disembodied feel as the record. As the band start the final ascending cacophony, I turn with back to the audience, and begin conducting the rising crescendo. If you can pull out all the stops on an electric organ, Rob is doing so. The cheers that greet his final devastating chord do not wither and die into the canvass surround, but ring on... giving us pause to recover before launching into "Hello Goodbye" in front of a sea of bouncing heads.

In the final extended chorus of "Hey Jude" we pull our usual stunt of stopping the music and turning the microphone onto the audience. They respond like the Liverpool Kop, inflating the marquee with hot breath in the mild July night... and there, standing in the middle, as the house lights flood the tent and blanch the white faces that frame hundreds of simultaneously manouvering tongues and gums, stands Nicky Byrne. The man who won and lost a fortune for John, Paul, George and Ringo, his eyes dewy in rememberance, has his arms aloft like an Evangelist, leading the crowd to the Promised Land. Sentimental old sod that I am, I have to compose myself before rejoining the chorus. The sunglasses have proved their worth tonight.

From "Jude" on, it's all rock'n'roll. When John and I both execute a Pete Townshend style scissor-kick to complete "Back in the USSR", I realise we may just be getting a little carried away with this rock star business. What with his back and my tight trousers, we're certainly taking a few risks tonight. Mr Eccentric MC leaps up on the stage to announce that we've got seven minutes left before the local council uproot all the power lines and the police place us all under arrest. With no chance for an encore, we run headlong into "She Loves You" followed by "Twist and Shout" which guarantees the band a raucous reception and me a sore throat.

We wave goodbye like real celebrities and slip into the

backstage area. I hug Rob and Taff, John hugs Lester and before we know it, we're standing in a linked circle bouncing up and down to a swift chorus of "Ole, Ole" before coming to our senses and realising that we don't do that sort of thing.

Nicky wanders in to give his thanks and the man from the press gives every indication that the review might be worth getting out of bed for on Monday morning. An events promoter and a roustabout both look eager to get us on their respective circuits and the organisers fail to short change us by fifty quid. All in all, a night to remember.

July 17th

It was never going to be easy following last night. John and Jane are teachers at Millfield and make a lovely couple. The wedding reception is running late as usual and we cannot unload the gear until tables are cleared. The Spanish style villa incorporating a hotel and vineyard between Wells and Glastonbury is also going to give us acoustic hell due to the heavy emphasis on terracotta tile.

Further complications are created by the fact that many of the guests also attended the Kingweston Ball and could be forgiven for being unenthusiastic about seeing us twice in eight days.

No doubt we are all tired from giving everything the night before. I am doubly incapacitated however, when I experience what I can only imagine was an asthma attack whilst driving across the Mendips. The hayfever appears to have dried up this year but other symptoms seem to be taking the place of the itchy throat and monumental sneezing fits. The sudden seizure brings out the very worst of my tendencies to hypochondria. I naturally think I am going to die and overreact by hyperventilating. I arrive at the vineyard feeling in need of a good lie down, preferably in the back of an ambulance. The delay in setting up, gives me an hour to recover and apart from the odd falsetto squeaking through my dusty tubes, the performance is little affected. John and Jane take their leave with "Hey Jude", although to follow their departure with "Get Back" might have been a touch insensitive on our part. Not a classic gig but at least we manage to get through the evening without having to make excuses or apologies.

July 19th

Rise early. Still feeling wheezy. Anne insists I go to the dreaded doctors. The Health Centre line is permanently engaged. Eventually I drive up and queue for an appointment. Predictably I have to return to emergency surgery at 4.30.

Pick up the *Western Daily Press*. No sign of a picture or write-up, despite phoning me three times yesterday for more details. I assume it must be confined to the Wiltshire edition and drive three miles across the border by Longleat to buy another copy. It's not in that version either.

4.30 p.m

Emergency surgery has drawn a crowd bigger than the average attendance at the Cheese and Grain Hall. I ask if I can make an appointment for tomorrow: "Yes. But you'll have to phone in the morning." Thence comes my fit again.

July 20th

Chest still feeling like a seasoned sixty-a-day multi-tar, full strength, untipped Woodbine smoker with pleurisy. Well... a bit wheezy anyway. Phone the doctors. The earliest appointment they have is for 8.50 tomorrow morning. Hoping I do not die before then, I eagerly accept the offer.

Head across the border to collect *Western Daily Press* (West Wilts edition). Two separate large close-ups of John and I, sweating profusely with moustache make-up trailing like dribble. The paper chooses to highlight the "look-a-like" angle. No review as such and Rob's name missed out of the line-up. It's fair to say we do look like two of The Beatles, though which two is anybody's guess.

TV debut day for Sgt Pepper's Only Dart Board Band. Having appeared on the box a few times in the past, John and I are working hard to look very cool and underwhelmed by the whole business. Nonetheless, a twinge of excitement and an inflated sense of self-importance lurks perilously close to the surface.

The show is called *The Pleasure Guide* and goes out across the region at 5.30 on Friday afternoons, quietly fulfilling HTV's commitment to local programmes without actually harming the viewing figures for *Neighbours* on the other channel. The format is that of a listings guide for forthcoming events. We are billed as "Special Guests" although "officially" they are giving us free airtime to plug our show at The Rondo in Bath on Saturday. This allows the flexibility of not having to pay us.

Full advantage is therefore made of the company's hospitality lunch and we ensure our plates are copiously overflowing with every conceivable and irrational combination of delicacies. We greatly relish not having to change in a toilet and the idea of having our moustaches artistically applied by an extremely attractive professional has the boys queuing up outside make-up slavering in anticipation.

The show is hosted by Graham Purches, a tall, well-chiselled veteran of West Country news and current affairs broadcasting. Graham, who also produces the show is terribly nice if quite earnest, worrying a little about our pre-song interview. When John and I persuade him that we want to do the whole thing in role with lots of Beatle irony, he says it sounds great. We run a couple of responses past him including, "We used to be on LSD but now we're on Viagra", but he looks at us perplexed, before belatedly forcing a chuckle:

"Ah yes, Viagra... I get it. Of course. Ha ha. You see, when you said LSD, I was thinking of pounds shillings and pence. I thought you were going to say 'but now were prefer the Euro... or something.'"

Clearly, years of being Bristol's answer to Kent Brockman has taken its toll. We decide to eliminate the joke.

In make-up, we meet co-presenter Gill Impey who is going through some intense artistic decision-making over the adoption of a very elaborate hair-do. Gill is the young, trendy, blonde little scamp to Graham's straight man. Graham is so straight in fact, he makes Sid Little look the master of urbane wit. Lester imagines Graham modelling cardigans in a Grattan's catalogue. What he imagines Gill modelling is better left unsaid.

Graham and the team have reluctantly accepted our determination to do a live recording. They would much preferred us to mime but we declined to go to the trouble, even in John's home studio, of creating a backing track. To us, the live sound has become a point of principle and one that gives our set an edge and spontaneity some other tribute bands lose. Last week, a technician from a staging company told me, while discussing plans for next year's Clark's beanfeast, how one of their roadies had depped on bass for a very prominent Abba tribute. When I suggested he must have been bloody good to do so at a moment's notice, it was revealed that the entire show was recorded on click track and that they simply programmed in the bass line and the guy just mimed. Adopting this formula would necessitate having to decide exactly how many choruses of a song like "Hey Jude" to sing; where to let the audience join in and for how many bars – and to make sure any spontaneous solos were firmly eradicated. I cannot imagine anything more emasculating.

Anyway, I digress... Having insisted on a live recording we

are determined not to cock-up. The crew is very impressed by our advanced preparation and the whole thing is done in a couple of takes. A rough playback gives us a good idea of how it will come out and while the others are putting in suggestions for sound balance, I am inevitably scrutinising the wig in case anyone can see the join in close-up. The old, soon-to-be-replaced Pepper uniforms look surprisingly good under the studio lights. I have no confidence, however, that come Friday, the backroom boys won't have remodelled us in the guise of a tinny sounding, tacky looking semi-finalists in the weekly talent competition at Butlin's, Minehead.

July 21st

Doctor's appointment at 8.50 in the morning and he's already behind schedule. Lung capacity good but clearly a touch of allergic asthma. Prescribes a sinus spray. It's the nearest I'll ever get to snorting before a show.

July 23rd

Colour photos in the *Bath Evening Chronicle* and *Wiltshire Times,* though the latter brilliantly manages to confuse John with me and me with Lester. The review of the Woolley show is superb considering it was based on rumour and conjecture rather than accurate observation. *The Pleasure Guide* broadcast completes a week of media saturation for the Dart Board Band. Apart from Graham Purches's incisive questioning: ("Now you're supposed to be Paul, but I keep thinking you're George, why is that?") the feature looks and sounds very good as long as you don't keep playing it repeatedly on video. Gill Impey's off-camera sing-along is only barely audible and when the camera pans across to our two presenters clapping along, Graham displays all the natural rhythm of Herman Munster.

Given that promoters seem quite impressed by our one camera amateur video from the Octagon Theatre, Yeovil; we quietly hope this appearance will help sell us to a more lucrative market.

July 24th

The lucky listeners of GWR radio who phoned in to win two tickets for our show at The Rondo, do not show up. The press are also absent. I know this because The Rondo is a small and intimate theatre and absconders' empty seats stand out like gaps in a toothy smile.

Senior citizens make up a larger than usual proportion of tonight's "full house." The pace is slower with much more emphasis on the jokes and audience banter. Eventually we break down the polite atmosphere and soon get the insults flying back and forth across the footlights.

Hopefully this will be the last time we wear the current costumes. The heavy bandsman's uniforms are due to be replaced by lighter, bright satin-type Sgt Pepper uniforms similar to those worn by John and myself. The bandsman's outfits looked good behind the three of us up front but the smaller line-up demands that we all look the same. The coats worn by John and me have seen four years of military service and with our increasing weight and a degree of natural shrinkage, Rob is right in suggesting we should release an album entitled "Flabby Road".

Mike Cole, the artist introduced after The Bell gig, turned up to take photos before the show which we may use on a projected live souvenir album in the future. His idea of parodying Beatles album covers has led to a rush of potential CD titles. Apart from the aforementioned "Flabby Road", in which we would be seen on a zebra crossing as it is being painted by an unsuspecting Paul McCartney; we also liked the idea of an absurdly elongated close-up of our heads under the title "Rubber Pants". *Revolver* would naturally become "Revolting" and a double album in a dark brown cover would also be available and commonly referred to as

"The Shite Album". We quite fancied "The Tragical History Tour" but The Rutles beat us to it by about twenty years.

The Rondo brings a lively end to a hectic summer schedule. We decided to devote August to family holidays, which is just as well as no one has made us a decent offer anyway.

In the last two months we have turned around the potentially disastrous departures of Steve and Mike and played some of the best gigs in the three years since this line-up came together. Last week, John met an old contact in the recording business who, having seen us at Woolley, was surprised to discover John was our Paul McCartney. "I've seen The Bootleg Beatles twice," he said, "but you're better." Forgive me for a well-earned gloat.

The Idiot's Guide... No: 7
A Day in the Life

During the period after The Beatles finished touring, John Lennon seemed to spend much of his time in bed. Whilst McCartney was quenching his thirst for art and culture in London, Lennon stewed in the sleepy stockbroker suburbs of Surrey. Now in Surrey, if you don't take up golf, semi-retirement can lead to a very insular life. Lennon was never likely to follow the footsteps of his old boyhood chum Jimmy Tarbuck around the bunkers of the pro-celebrity circuit, so he continued writing and experimenting with recordings.

Amazingly, from this rather dull, unadventurous period, many exceptional songs were born. "I'm Only Sleeping", like The Kinks' "Sunny Afternoon" and "Lazy Sunday Afternoon" by The Small Faces, is evocative of the relaxed and laid back late sixties lifestyle. If Lennon found inspiration in sleeping then this was surpassed when he churned out "Good Morning, Good Morning" after watching a TV ad for cornflakes. Both songs used atmospheric sounds to good effect and this development in his work achieved brilliance with re-working the words of an old Victorian show poster into "Being for the Benefit of Mr. Kite". We used to do "Mr. Kite" in the set. Mike (and before him Nigel Mintram) sang it in a declamatory style like a circus ring master, which seemed perfectly appropriate in the stage show *All You Need is Love*. Out of context, this version struggled to impress the tanked up, bar-room brawlers we later attempted to entertain and so "Mr. Kite" was dropped from the bill. "Bloody good," said Steve Hurd, "I hate that bloody song."

Continuing in the vein of drawing inspiration from the mundane, Lennon came up with a mournful tune based around newspaper reports and called it "A Day in the Life". Paul McCartney welded into the song a middle section about getting up, getting on the bus, having a fag and wanting to turn us all on. It seems McCartney saw the potential for orchestration and George Martin assembled a highly trained string and brass section. Paul then instructed them to play from their lowest note to their highest in their own time. He also dressed them in comedy noses.

The result was one of the most unforgettable moments in rock music, although the style is no more of a pop song than Bach's "Toccata and Fugue". The percussion punctuates the lines of verse rather than maintaining the beat. The piano is the dominant instrument, maintaining a simple descending chord progression with gravity and pomp. The words are powerful, moving and yet abstract and distant, Lennon's voice mixed back almost as if we are hearing it on a radio news bulletin or down a phone line. When the sound effect of the alarm clock is heard, it is as if he has been woken from a dream. The McCartney section then ends with "somebody spoke and I fell into a dream" and we are back floating into "Four thousand holes in Blackburn Lancashire".

How the hell do you recreate this masterpiece on stage? It would be most tempting to use a pre-recorded click track but we prefer to keep the show wholly live. Rob manages to reproduce the strings effectively and the climbing orchestral cacophony is achieved by guitars working out of time against one another and the keyboard. Lennon's distant, nasal vocal cannot be easily impersonated live but a good sound engineer will be able to swamp the vocals with reverb creating a similar effect. When learning this song, for some reason we used four voices on the "aaaah" section that links McCartney's piece with the final verse. The record simply has Lennon in plaintive echo. The four voices in harmony create a climax which abruptly contrasts with the re-introduction of the "I read the news today" theme. During our occasional concerts with choirs we have found that the introduction of thirty voices singing the "aaaahs" is spine tingling.

As with so much of the Dart Board Band set, what is lost in subtlety can be compensated for in sheer energy and initiative. "A Day in the Life" usually segues on from "Lucy in the Sky With Diamonds" which presents the same problem for the vocal sound. With the help of the audience joining in the choruses however, a momentum builds which carries through "A Day in the Life" and makes this section of the show perhaps the most satisfying. The tumultuous ending with the eternal piano chord has often been greeted in open-mouthed silence by the audience. I hope it's because they are impressed rather than appalled. Perhaps I should ask.

August

August 3rd

A month off. Perhaps I should spare you details of our brief period of rest? Sorry, but you don't get off that lightly.

Today, I receive a call from Trina, the assistant to the corporate events man who approached us at the Woolley Festival. Usually these vague promises amount to nothing so I am surprised to be engaged in the following conversation:

TRINA: Are you available on February 9th? That's a Wednesday.

ME: (*Tentatively*). Yes... at the moment. What's it for?

TRINA: A conference. Medical industry jolly.

ME: How much?

TRINA: Well... how much do you usually charge?

ME: (*Trying not to sound too naive*). Well... to be honest we don't usually do corporates. I mean we don't have an agent to put them our way. What's the venue?

TRINA: It's actually a big museum like the Exploratory in Bristol.

ME: Right. Where is it?

TRINA: Edinburgh.

ME: Edinburgh? (*Pause*). Look I'm going to have to level with you here. We've all got day jobs. It would mean taking time off. That's going to present big problems.

TRINA: Can you take holiday?

ME: Well, two of us are teachers. The holidays are set in tablets of stone.

TRINA: Well, I've been told try and pencil you in. The boss loved your act at the festival.

ME: Look. I'll get back to you. I'll ring them tonight.

Taff and Rob are cautious about dedicating too much holiday to work after taking the day off recently to record the HTV thing. John and I know that only an act of gross deception will cover our absence from work and will not be worth the risk. Lester's all for it though. He suggests that, if the money was good enough, we could fly up. I get onto Bristol Airport. Knowing that one can fly from Luton for less than forty quid, I am horrified to be quoted a fare in excess of three hundred. I get back to Trina:

ME: Look, this Edinburgh gig. The only way we could do it is by flying up and back the following morning. It's three hundred plus per person. We'd also need equipment set up for us at the other end.

TRINA: Three hundred? We can get you up there for much less. We've got an arrangement with BA.

ME: But I thought you'd probably only pay for a van or something.

TRINA: No. We'd fly you up there. We're flying most of the delegates up there.

ME: What about the equipment?

TRINA: Well, there's four other bands going up there. We can organise that for you. I mean, we've shipped stuff out to places like Dubai in the past. Let's have a look at flight times. (*Furious tapping of computer keys heard in the background.*)

Yea. We could fly you out on the five thirty. The first flight back is ...seven in the morning. That should get you into work alright. It takes ninety minutes.

ME: What about the fee?

TRINA: I don't know. You needn't worry. It'll be worth your while. Can I pencil you in?

ME: Oh, go on then.

Sgt Pepper's Only Dart Board Band

I put the phone down wondering what the hell I'm doing. This is big time. Well, it's big time compared to the Black Swan at Trowbridge anyway.

I phone Lester to break the good news. It is at this point I remember my hatred of flying and start to imagine what kind of conditions might accompany a journey to Scotland in mid-winter. I ask Lester to promise me he won't ever suggest we incorporate a Buddy Holly set in the show.

August 4th

Neon Monkey appear at the Cheese and Grain at an "Unsigned Bands Night". This is promoted by Richard, the owner of the Raves From The Grave record shop who is also finding it tough to deal with the hall management.

As John and I enter, we point out that we're with the band. Colin the technician immediately responds, "That's funny I thought you said you were banned!" I hesitantly enquire if he's being serious or not. He assures me that although many have been banned, we are not yet on the list. I am anxious to know if I will have to avoid eye contact with the hall manager tonight. "I doubt it very much," he says, rolling a ciggy. "She's on three week's holiday. Before that she was off for a month with stress." And I thought I had good holidays.

Being local, the boys go up last, following a couple of bands in their late teens. The first, Aleus are musically very competent and sport a frontman who clearly fancies himself as a bit of a Jim Morrison with his tight hipsters and sixties haircut. The sound balance is not helped by an audience of only fifty to soak up the cavernous echo. The second band, Edible Decorations, gig regularly and have great presence as well as writing some good songs that would come across with deserved clarity in a more appropriate setting. They look very confident and assured and I sense that they may be capable of succeeding in the business.

Neon Monkey have a tough act to follow and Tom and

Richard's little amps are dwarfed on the high stage. Tom is at full volume to compete with the acoustics and Colin's selective miking of bass and drums. It is evident that their confidence is growing with every gig. Head banging and Townshend type leaps get the sedate audience behind them. They now need to include a few songs of their own to make the next step forward. It is heart-warming to think that when John and I finally decide we are too old to be throwing ourselves around onstage, we might actually make our fortunes by working for the boys. As John Lennon once said in answer to the question, "What's the secret of your success?"

"If we knew the answer to that, we'd give up and become managers."

August 11th

Total Eclipse. Well, 97.5% in Somerset, which is about 97.5% better than in Cornwall where totality is masked by 100% cloud cover. The dark, eerie, midday gloom turned out to be slightly less intrusive than a wet afternoon in November. The eclipse, Nostradamus's supposed predictions and the approaching Millennium are giving the doom-mongers a productive time.

August 18th

Simon Horsey and wife Sonia are back from Saudi for the summer. Simon wrote the music for my plays *Defectors* and *An Audience with Ben Jonson* as well as being the original keyboard player on *All You Need is Love* and Who Two. The Ben Jonson piece appeared at the Café Royal in the Edinburgh Fringe Festival three years ago. Simon says he knows a bloke who might be interested in the latter. I retrieve my old Amstrad computer from the loft and run off a faint copy. This inspires some frantic follow-up work. I write to remind John Broome at the Shakespeare Festival Theatre in Canada that he was going to try to produce a rehearsed reading of the script during their current season. I then make belated approaches to one or two publishers.

In the process of wading through old material I alight on a copy of *Waterloo Sunset*. Reading it again, I realise that with a few cuts here and there, the piece still has potential. The only trouble is getting Ray Davies to ever agree to release copyright. I start wondering whether an original score could replace the Kinks' hits. I start to scribble a possible opening number. It sounds reasonable without being reminiscent of any particular Davies composition. I move on to the next song cue. Within three days I have composed seven new songs. I haven't tried writing songs for years but the muse is flowing. Amazingly, I somehow manage to avoid the new songs sounding anything like their counterparts. I then realise this is due to the fact I am using a style heavily influenced by Lennon and McCartney. But then, so was Ray Davies.

August 28th
Return from a week in the Isle of Wight. I cannot begin to explain how twenty members of our family managed to be on the Island at the same time. The authorities were probably on invasion alert.

A strange experience. So little has changed since we first moved from London to our little house in Godshill twenty years ago this month. Whilst it was moving to be looking at Medina High School again and checking out our other old haunts, being a tourist increased one's sense of detachment.

The Island seems even more dependent on pensioners for its tourist trade then ever before. Paul Price remarked that at his hotel, he and Cheryl were the only ones eating dinner with their own teeth.

One thing that has certainly changed however, is the provision for entertainment. Sandown Pavilion, formerly a nine

Being John Lennon

hundred seat theatre, once a pillar of seaside variety featuring the likes of Norman Wisdom and Lennon's old chum Jimmy Tarbuck, was last year converted into an enormous amusement arcade. The seaside shows at Shanklin are shadows of their former selves and Ryde Pavilion is now a bowling alley. The Medina Theatre still runs a modest programme but opening the Anthony Minghella Theatre also in Newport, seems like a bad case of overkill.

The Prince Consort Theatre Club has now become some kind of night club/gymnasium complex. It was here, in 1982, I played Frank Spencer. The old Town Hall in Ryde, as if to compensate for this decline, has been re-christened a theatre. I am very tempted to try for a booking with Sgt Pepper next year, if only to get to see those parts of the island inaccessible to a fleet of cars from Luton.

A part of me would have loved to have produced a programme to have saved at least one of these theatres. Of course the programme might also have been an excuse for a massive personal ego-trip.

There, that was most of August. Wasn't so painful after all, was it?

The Idiot's Guide... No:8
Hello Goodbye

The Beatles made a virtue of simple lyrics and catchy refrains. "Yellow Submarine" seemed to start the trend, followed by "All You Need is Love". This sing-a-long style reached its nemesis with "Na, na, na (etc. etc.) Hey Jude!" John and Yoko of course, carried on the tradition with "Give Peace a Chance" to the extent that we wished they would.

"Hello Goodbye" has a lyric which may seem complex by the standards of McCartney's "All Together Now" on the *Yellow Submarine* soundtrack, but is basically utter nonsense. The song has a wonderful driving momentum though, which is sustained by the backing vocals singing a counter melody. Fortunately for John, Lester and Taff, this is sung an octave lower than the top line which is my pleasure to attempt. McCartney had such a high voice in his youth which didn't always hold out in middle age. I thought nothing would stretch my range as much as impersonating Roger Daltrey but at least with The Who you can open out the throat and scream a bit. With Paul's vocals they are high of pitch and very controlled. Take the middle eight of "A Hard Day's Night"... I wish you would, 'cause I can't. Not in the original key anyway. That "When I'm home" line is hard enough but "feeling you holding me tight, tight, yeah" requires nothing less than a tight, tight grip on the testicles, yeah.

"Hello Goodbye" is also one of several songs that demand a creative ending by their use of fade out on the original recording. "Hello Goodbye" appears to finish naturally, only to introduce the repeated refrain of "Haila, hail hello" (or however it's meant to be spelled). When we've had enough "hailas" with a nod and a wink we go back into a reprise of the chorus. This is meant to be seamless, but occasionally we don't read the nods and winks all at the same time. It's better than counting bars though, and means you can judge the audience response before curtailing the community singing. It's also good if you've had enough and want to get home early. Thank-you, Hello and Goodbye...

September

Sept 4th

I have discovered the dark secret behind the Conservative Party's success. How can a political movement whose main philosophy seems to be to create obscene wealth for the few at the expense of the many, have such an unwavering bed-rock of support amongst those it appears to exploit?

The answer lies deep in a working class district of Poole, where there exists what is to all intents and purposes a traditional working men's club. An enormous room with a series of snooker tables at one end, bays of padded vinyl seats and a lengthy bar, serves to accommodate a considerable body of regulars. Many are elderly, mixing without reserve, amongst the younger, drunker and less respectable element. A substantial dance floor with a stage in one corner serves to create a barrier between the revellers and those who would seek to entertain them.

Tonight, it is Sgt Pepper's Only Dart Board Band's chance to lead this particular horse to water. Unfortunately the horse is so inebriated that it cannot reach the trough without stopping at the nearby saloon. And herein lies the secret of the Tory's mystical influence over a sizeable minority of the British proletariat. The beer at these clubs is substantially subsidised. The multinational brewers, some well known for their support of the Party, help provide ale to the fully paid up member at the enviably generous price of one pound per pint. The political knock-on effect is manifestly clear:

Being John Lennon

Having lured in Handsel and Gretel Public into their parlour, the unsuspecting entrants are suitably tranquillised and fattened by the tempting range of beverages at prices that won't soak up the entire Family Allowance. During elections the Tories can then rest assured of one of the following responses from their club members:

A) Fearing that lack of support will close their beloved drinking den, members will, in desperation, vote Conservative.

Or...

B) Members will be so drunk as to forget that Mrs Thatcher made them unemployable for ten years.

Or...

C) Members inclined to vote for other parties won't even be able to stagger to the nearest polling station.

Given that less than half a dozen were able even to stagger to the dance floor, the above suggestions do not seem entirely unreasonable. After a month off, it is fair to say the band is a little rusty but frankly, most of this audience wouldn't notice if we were as rotten as a pear. By the second half we crank up the volume having reassured the Social Secretary that the enthusiastic response he witnessed at The Silent Whistle would be repeated. I stretch my mic lead as far into the audience as decency will allow on "Hey Jude" and briefly awaken the comatose for a few rousing choruses. For once, "Get Back" fails to do the trick. Those vinyl seats are like adhesive to arses ballasted by beer. Having given my vocal chords the old cheese cutter treatment on "With A Little Help From My Friends", I hit the heights of "Drive My Car" forgetting that after a month's inactivity my throat is not prepared for this bombardment. Suddenly, the voice snaps like an athlete pulling up with a torn hamstring. I had forgotten how much exercise it takes to sustain our two-hour set of gravelly rock and castrato warbles.

Mildly disappointing for the few who are bothering to listen, we cut the set short as I croak like a dying frog through "Twist and Shout".

After the high spots of the summer, this kind of gig may be what we need to bring us back to reality. Suitably chastised, we squeeze into the three cars and head off on the long trip home. As if to add insult to injury however, all three of us fall foul of the inconsistent signposting coming out of Poole and fail to appreciate the probable beauties of Wareham Forest at midnight. Rob, anxious to make up for lost time, manages also to get caught on a speed camera.

At least Lester got back from his holiday in time.

Sept 10th

The Bacon Theatre, Cheltenham is an Elizabethan inspired design situated in the plush grounds of Dean Close School. On the morning of the show I am informed that sales are low and that the house is being "papered" (i.e. free tickets are being distributed). I am not overly concerned as we are on a straight fee but with a deposition from Clark's coming to assess our suitability for their anniversary event, it would be better if we were seen to be a big draw.

As it's the first Friday into term, I'm pushed to get there for the six o'clock get in. I ask the others to lead the advance party in the hope of arriving soon after. The Friday rush hour through Bath is safely navigated but a serious hold up awaits on the A46. Ambulances and police cars race ominously past the stationary traffic. Gradually the queue crawls towards the cause of the delay. An articulated lorry lies overturned on the roadside verge. The driver, lying quite still alongside his cab is receiving oxygen. No other vehicle seems to have been affected. The scene sends a vibrant shudder through me and I vow not to race too impatiently through the quaint Cotswold settlements that line the route. My vow probably lasts ten minutes. As I approach Cheltenham through the cliff edged roads south of the town, the mobile rings. Rob and John, far from being ahead of me, have chosen another route, have been delayed and have forgotten where we are playing. With the line cracking up as I attempt to navigate the long and winding road down into the town one handed, I find myself shouting impatiently: "No...no...not *Bean* Close...*Dean* Close School! That's D.E... Yes *Dean* Close. No, *D* for Dennis... No, it's nothing to do with Tennis! Oh, for Christ's sake!"

I arrive at the scene to find a worried looking technician peering through the door. It turns out I am the first to arrive. On Tuesday at rehearsal I had issued clear details to the rest of the band as to location and times. I am, to say the least, upset and embarrassed by this lack of professionalism. The fact that I had a further 25 miles to travel indicates just how late the others are by comparison. I try contacting Stuart on his mobile. It is switched off. It once again confirms my suspicion that communication technology actually increases stress rather than convenience. I manage to bottle my feelings when John and Rob arrive, not wishing to create a negative atmosphere before the gig. We set up as best we can assuming Lester and Stuart are not too far behind.

With fifteen minutes to curtain up, Rob, John and I apply costume and make-up and begin to discuss what to do in the event of Lester and Taff's non-arrival. Rob and I are for busking a few quiet numbers to borrow time. John is adamantly opposed, taking the view that we should cancel. This exemplifies the fundamental difference between us as performers. As indicated previously, John wishes to be thoroughly prepared for performance, leaving nothing to chance. Whilst applauding that virtue, I love the spontaneity of live performance and enjoy the danger of improvisation. This difference could easily develop into a full-blown argument. We decide to defer the decision and I return to Taff's mobile number, quietly imploring his recorded message service to somehow instruct him to switch the bloody thing on. At that point, Lester's old Volvo leaps over the school speed ramps and with all hands to the pump we complete the fastest recorded get-in in theatre history. At two minutes past eight with the audience still struggling to their seats, Lester and Taff, sweating profusely, make final adjustments to their costumes and the curtain opens to reveal a full house of 500. Most of them are school pupils on a free invite but there is significantly more adults and "public" than we were, at first, led to expect.

Despite a not unsurprising nervy start, the show is a considerable improvement on the last and after enthusiastic encores we don't get offstage until 10.40. Little remains to be said about the delay. Once again the Dart Board Band escapes by the skin of its teeth.

Sept 18th

Another spin off from our leafy Hertfordshire appearances. This wedding reception is a particularly opulent number in a large marquee set in the grounds of the bride's parents' unostentatious but attractive home on the Herts/Essex border. After last week, I think it better not to risk travelling in convoy to this remote backwater and manage to borrow a school minibus with ample boot space for the occasion.

As with our previous trip in a mini-bus, inclement weather makes driving less pleasant and as the only permitted driver I soon begin to question my decision to act as tour guide. True to form, Lester and John are unconscious within five minutes of leaving Frome. Lester has a hangover from spending the previous evening watching Steve and The Skreechers at a local pub and John is heavily sedated on painkillers

Being John Lennon

thanks to a mouth abscess and an attack of facial neuralgia. I start to wonder if they will survive an evening in which we are due to further extend the act with a final set of rock standards.

As it happens the cast hold up better than the bus which starts registering a thermostat problem just as we arrive and leaves us pondering throughout the gig the likelihood of our successful return to Somerset. The hosts, Dean and Pippa make sure we are well looked after and the caterer Jenny, treats us like royalty. As we stuff in the stuffed salmon, John enquires of Lester (between bouts of abscess antagonised agony) as to whether The Skaters were given such respect yesterday evening. Lester replies that they may have shared a complimentary bag of Porky Scratchings, but he couldn't be sure. Given that this is one of our highest paid gigs to date, Lester's seemingly self-effacing comment that he didn't "want to crow" but he saw them being "slipped a few quid" at the end of the evening, brings howls of cynical laughter. He also mentions that The Skeemers would like to come with us to Germany next year. John is momentarily anaesthetised with shock. "If they go Lester, I don't," he snarls through clenched teeth and half-chewed salmon. I surmise that Lester must be a suffering short-term brain damage due to a combination of loud music and alcohol ingestion.

The gig signals another improvement but the ring rust has yet to fully rub off. The caterer's generosity knows no bounds with booze and food flowing in from all angles during the breaks and at the end of the evening. John, high on a cocktail on champagne, painkillers and penicillin shows little sign of allowing another glass or two to stand between him and a stomach pump. Lester meanwhile, is downing them like a stag weekend veteran. Unfortunately a combination of circumstances leads our host Dean, to surmise that we are having it away with more of the Chateau Neuf du Pape than is our due.

September 19th - 7 PM.

Arrived home a six o'clock this morning having aquaplaned the bus through the flooding highways of the West Country whilst keeping a watchful eye on the temperature gauge and willing the engine not to blow up. Rob and Taff make a sterling effort to stay awake so as to ensure that I do the same. Both fail. John rapidly slips into a deep coma. Lester, when not accusing Taff of slipping barbiturates into his drink is snoring loudly. We unload the bus to discover a speaker stand, a microphone and Rob's trousers are missing.

I awake at midday, still tired. The house is subdued. Anne proceeds to tell me that there is a problem with Tom. She then bursts into tears. My mind races with fears and anxiety. "Don't worry," she says, "it's just that he's shaved all his hair off." An explanation as to how he was overpowered by a moment of daring and a "friend" with hair clippers, ensues. I storm into his room and demand he remove the hat the hides the offending head. He reveals a penis-like dome topped off by a Mohican crest. This is the latest and most bizarre in a series of ridiculous hair styles which have generally failed to offend our sixties liberal sensitivities. Today however, I am reduced to a few choice expletives before rushing out in a mist of anger. Apologies are later made and reassurances given that he will not return home with a tattoo, eyebrow piercing, navel stud or any other form of decorative self-abuse without consulting us first.

I phone Dean and Pippa to enquire as to whereabouts of missing trousers etc. I apologise for the possible misconception concerning freeloading. Pippa is very kind in pointing out that yes, something was mentioned but they had a lovely time and we needn't worry, no offence was taken.

Tea time: Pricey phones. Having set us up with the gig,

he's got wind of the freeloading story. Apparently Dean was so pleased with our work he was going to tip us another hundred quid on top of the already sizeable fee. Naturally enough, the sight of a certain band members staggering to the bus under the weight of bottles concealed and bottles drunk, left him, as well as the offending members, with a bitter aftertaste. The tip was withheld. I feel I must formally write to apologise. The irony is, of course, that *I* was sober as a judge having taken on the driving duties. We've got to learn that professionalism occurs on and off the stage.

The weekend has ended on a downer. I try to console myself with the fact that a contract has arrived for the publication of the play *An Audience with Ben Jonson*. The publisher specialises in Scottish Plays. After three years of postponing sending the script to anyone, the first company I try has gone for it. Maybe I should reconsider my future.

September 23rd

Pippa phones at school distraught to have received my grovelling letter and stating that the whole matter has been blown out of proportion. I dread to think what this conversation must have sounded like to the eavesdropping pupils in my room at the time. Anyway, this makes it a lot easier to confront the lads tonight at The Riverside, Bradford on Avon.

The issue is dealt with diplomatically and they seem to regret the interpretation of events. I express the view that even in the circumstances, a bit of caution might have been appropriate. I hate sounding like a teacher when out of school but what annoyed me more than the missing tip is the fact that several potential customers took our cards and we shouldn't have compromised hard-earned bookings.

The Riverside is very quiet. A couple of Glaswegian refrigerator repair men staying at the hotel come in to the junk/dressing room in the interval to buy us drinks. Despite the tepid atmosphere, they're loving it. One guy, Archie, says: "I've seen the Bootlegs – you'se lot is betta than they are, I can tell ye!" This gives us considerable lift for the second half. It's not the number but the response of the audience that counts.

September 21ˢᵗ

I've recently been engaging in a bit of banter on *Tribute Band Mania* web site. The organisers are running a competition to find "The World's Favourite Tribute Band" which has brought a flood of messages onto their notice board. I cannot help but join in by voting for the Dart Board Band. My initial message accuses an American Beatles tribute called Revolution of getting their mates to clog up the web-site. I counter that we are the best in the world and that listening to our CDs like "Flabby Road", "Rubber Pants" and "The Shite Album" proves the point. I also ask Revoltion (a fortuitous miss-type) how their Scouse accents are coming on. This provokes a response from someone by the name of Ringo moaning in phonetic Yankee Scouse about "Limeys clogging up the web site" and referring to us as "wankaeus." I register a vote in my son Richard's name with a message suggesting that he is being forced into supporting his father in this event. Afraid of being disqualified for voting too much from one address, I ask Tom Sangster to give us his vote. More than one vote should at least get our name off the bottom of the list.

A bloke referring to himself as Keef from Sticky Fingers, a Hollywood-based Stones tribute, writes in stating how much he looks forward to listening to "Flabby Road". I begin to get the impression that the humorous approach has paid dividends over those sad, earnest, pleas for support that others have canvassed.

Today the results are published. The only UK Band in the top ten is The Royal Family, a Queen tribute who must have some kind of mailing list to motivate their fans into action. This is based on the premise that they can't be that big if they're regularly playing the Memorial Theatre in Frome. Top votes are in the hundred to two hundred mark with a rapid falling off outside the top ten. Somehow we have accrued the grand total of nine votes. This actually gives us a highly respectable chart position just outside the top twenty. More significantly however, we are second only to the Bootlegs (on a modest 29) amongst UK Beatle acts and fifth most popular Beatles tribute in the entire world. All based on nine votes. Surely, we can capitalise on this? After all, over twelve hundred votes were registered in all, making a credible sample. If I'd discovered the site a week earlier I could have manipulated a vote that would have reached double figures. The moral of this message: Never trust opinion polls.

PS: Revolution finished with only eight votes. Whoo hoo!

The Idiot's Guide...No:9 No:9 No:9 etc.: Revolution Number 9.

At one gig a young group of lads kept calling for songs from the *White Album*. When John Freeman responded with "OK, we'll do 'Revolution Number 9'", their eyes lit up in expectation. These boys were clearly serious addicts to Beatles music as well as a variety of exotic plants.

How much time Lennon actually spent assembling this rambling collection of sound effects, I don't know, but "Revolution Number 9" marks a low (or perhaps a "high") point in The Beatles pursuit of musical experimentation.

Having integrated sound effects into songs on the *Sgt Pepper* album, the idea of using random sounds unhindered by any musical content was symptomatic of Lennon's penchant for avant-garde art and McCartney's flirtation with "serious" contemporary music.

They weren't the only band in the "Summer of Love" using concepts, themes and sounds to link their songs. The *Sgt Pepper* album was actually being recorded back-to-back at the Abbey Road studios with Pink Floyd's *Piper at the Gates of Dawn* and the underrated *S.F. Sorrow* by the Pretty Things. The Beatles were always the first to anticipate a trend and *Sgt Pepper* with its lengthy studio time investment and marketing impact, was bound to overshadow the others. While *Pepper* used Peter Blake and Jann Howarth as pop-art cover designers, *Sorrow* made do with the sketches of Pretty Things vocalist Phil May.

Having taught Blake and Howarth's daughter at Frome College, I later taught May's artistically talented son, Paris, at Millfield. Sadly, I never met Phil May but would have loved to get his reaction on *S.F. Sorrow* which was not only under-funded and under-promoted at the time but was a seminal influence on later so-called "rock operas" like *Arthur* by The Kinks and the immensely successful *Tommy* by The Who.

Sgt Pepper proved that The Beatles as a songwriting partnership, could produce consistent and brilliant compositions but could not sustain a theme or story as originally intended. The *Pepper* concept was quickly dropped in the studio but other, less diverse and creative composers like Pete Townshend actually found their talent expanded and stretched by working to a narrative structure.

By the time we get to the *White Album*, as stunning as some of the tracks are, the wheels are beginning to come off the Beatles bandwagon. They can be heard reverting to familiar rock formulas and parodying other musical styles. There seems less obvious song writing collaboration going on. Rough edges that would have been smoothed down in the past by the pride of a working partnership, are allowed to remain exposed in the final mix. McCartney seems happy not to condense "The Beatles" (as the album is actually called) into a single, unpadded, musical triumph. I mean, why did he and the others allow Ringo's "Don't Pass Me By" to go out at all, never mind with the "You were in a car crash and you lost your hair" line intact? Why didn't John give George a hand with that awful "sleeping/ sweeping" rhyme in the otherwise sublime "While My Guitar Gently Weeps?" And why couldn't George Martin persuade John to edit down (or preferably edit out) "Number 9"? This apparent tolerance of artistic indulgence would eventually lead to Paul, who appears keen to preserve The Beatles musical integrity, becoming the dominant partner in the *Abbey Road* and *Let it Be* sessions. The *White Album* sees all four Beatles pursuing individual agenda in their post-live performance period. It is the beginning of the end of the band.

No, of course we don't do "Revolution Number 9". It just wouldn't somehow go down at a wedding reception now would it? We do play "Revolution" though and "Back in the USSR," two of the more approachable tracks from the *White Album*. Interestingly, both highlight the Beatles gradual movement back to their rock'n'roll roots, the latter being a parody of the Beach Boys "Surfin' USA" which, in turn, was stolen from Chuck Berry. Paul and Mike Love collaborated on "Back in the USSR" whilst sunning themselves at the Maharishi's ashram in India. It's probably the only real collaboration on the album.

October

October 18th

Another month half-over and the newspapers are gearing themselves up for the big push to the Millennium. A lot of reflection has begun on this energetic, fearful century. A Millennium's worth of history is almost too much to contemplate but *The Guardian*'s Century supplement has begun to chronicle those familiar stories from the death of Victoria to the present day. What an awesome shadow the old Queen has cast over us. Down the years our Victorian forebears have made their sepia-toned imprint on our post-colonial past, looking proudly from old photos, defiantly upright and unquestioning. Even after the Second World War when the Empire began to dismantle, Victoria was eulogised by the Kinks and of course, The Beatles who (with the help of ex-Frome College parents Peter Blake and Jann Howarth) re-introduced Victoriana into pop art. Margaret Thatcher turned the 1980s into the 1890s as the embodiment of the 19th century matriarch calling for a return to Victorian values.

Driving back from Poole, Stuart and I diverted through the Dorset hills to Shaftesbury across Cranborne Chase where Hardy's Tess declined to cling to Alex D'Urberville as he swung the trap round its steep and perilously winding bends and turns.

Stuart and I had spent the night at The Central by invitation of the landlady. Ten pounds for a twin room seemed reasonable at the time but, on reflection, we might have asked for a refund. The room bore little resemblance to the authentic Victorian splendour of The Central's lounge bar. A broken plug on the TV, a dangerously exposed socket on the wall and an electricity meter which emitted blue sparks when touched, gave the room that "death trap" ambience. Once we had wrestled shut the sash window, we found the heater ineffective and thus spent the night curled up in our respective beds, shivering under the sheets. The cooked breakfast was a tempting inducement to stay a little longer but Taff and I decided to hit the road before frostbite set in.

The glorious journey alone justified the overnight stop and was a soothing antidote to the disappointing events of the night before. Although we played well, we had agreed to allow a local promoter to present us in the hope that he would increase our audience from the modest forty that turned up in June. He succeeded in reducing the total to twenty nine. His flyers managed to induce the willing punters to part with five quid by highlighting the fact that, during our first visit to The Central we had experienced "technical difficulties." Looking back over my account of that event, the "technical difficulties" amounted to no more than a slight imbalance in the sound that was remedied in the interval. The only person I heard complaining about it was the promoter himself. To be fair he dropped his cut to compensate, but driving to Poole for the grand sum of twenty four pounds each is hardly what you call a lucrative evening.

Worse still, Mr. Jones and colleague from Mr Jones' club came on complimentaries having booked us in at the Bournemouth venue in November. They left after three songs and have cancelled the arrangement. Despite an excellent reaction from the audience, we are apparently not right for Mr Jones' over-rated, rock-band rip-off sleaze-joint. Like

The Fleece in Bristol, these so-called "name venues" consider themselves important enough to hire and fire bands on a whim and completely cock-up their schedules. Yet the money they pay would be considered an insult if offered by a village primary school at a fund raising fete.

To add insult to injury, Clark's have dropped the idea of using tribute bands for their big anniversary next year and Terry at the Silent Whistle is packing off to Portugal. We've lost three out of four gigs in November and despite protestations that we can "really make it work at The Central," our position there is now untenable.

Last week we were back at Wolverhampton University, this time at their Telford Student Union Bar. We had a storming night, the students were superb and the fee generous. Just when I thought we might be returning to the heady success of the summer, the autumn breeze bites in.

October 23rd

The last time we played the Uptown Social Club in Corsham we arrived to find the manager had run off with the advanced ticket sales along with the Cancer Research charity box. A local hairdressers called Strawberry Fields had agreed to be an obvious ticket outlet for us but failed to sell a single ticket. Even the complementary tickets were given a resounding boycott. They still expected us to appear at their subsequent charity fashion show, mind you. Therein lies a typical example of the perils of charity shows. Despite keeping our half of the bargain we received not the slightest hint of thanks for our troubles.

The night at Corsham was memorable for our introduction to a clinically demented builder by the name of Dicky the Brickie. Dicky had arrived in a state of serious inebriation and continued to defy the law of gravity for the rest of the evening. At one point he stepped up to the microphone and simply stared at Mike Walker during "With a Little

Help From My Friends" with his eyeballs no more than six inches from the end of Mike's nose. His wife, somehow able to retain a sense of suburban dignity was so impressed with our restraint, she immediately booked us to reappear at her son's wedding.

Within minutes of arriving at the reception, Dicky bade me to converse with him face to face. Staring in tunnel vision like a pre-race Linford Christie, his opening gambit is:

"You don't remember me do you?" said in a sinister Clint Eastwood – I'm about to blow your brains out sort of way.

"Yes, I do. You were here before. You're the father of the groom aren't you?" I reply.

I hold my hand out. He refuses the gesture. A long Pinter-esque silence follows. Fearing he is about demonstrate the art of the head butt, I again attempt to break the ice.

"When do you want us to go on?" I enquire.

"Now!" came the reply.

"Well actually, it's only five past seven. I mean we can do two and a half hours but…"

"Now!" he reiterated with a chilling degree of assertion.

I didn't like to tell him that the bass player hadn't yet arrived. I blathered on about timings and finishing the evening on a high, all the time watching like a hawk to make sure he didn't reach for his revolver. Suddenly his mood changed:

"Can I get you lads a drink?" He put his arm round me and marched me off to the club bar where he proceeded to introduce himself as, "Dicky the Brickie, the best in the West, I fuck 'em and leave 'em and go on to the rest." He growled out this catch phrase in his hybrid Irish, country yokel accent at every available opportunity. My, how we laughed! Dicky made us laugh like he was the master of urbane wit. We dare not do otherwise. He then entertained us with a series of riddles. Lester was frighteningly switched on to Dicky's wavelength and endeared himself to our host by solving the riddles. Lester had already downed a couple of pints so he could see where Dicky was coming from.

So the evening wore on with Dicky one moment offering us drinks, the next accusing us of "taking the piss" for accepting. Thanks to his insistence on an early start, the best man organised a collection to induce us to play another set. We repeated our recent rock'n'roll encore from the famous "wedding of the missing wine" occasion and kept the audience on their feet until well after the agreed concluding time. Dicky was so impressed he tried to shake our hands as we played. John politely refused to attempt McCartney bass lines one handed. This caused great offence to Dicky who pointed at his temples and accused John of being "fucking mad". I personally would have dropped my new Rickenbacker copy on the dance floor to accept Dicky's hand of friendship.

Thinking he had found a soul mate, Dicky cornered Lester at the bar afterwards. Lester's report of the conversation went something like this:

DICKY: *(Running slurred words together)*. I thin... yer... suggin... in a placemat on the bylico of my doorstep.

LESTER: Oh yes?

DICKY: An if yer nuttin in the blandbush of wisteria from the troutstream of oblivion... Move yer van into a parkin bench of illicit demons.

LESTER: Exactly.

DICKY: And if yer chogwanna is laring in its petunias... Do me the dogwhistle of putting on a brace of pheasant.

LESTER: I couldn't agree more. You're absolutely right.

DICKY: Right? Right? Waddyafuckingmeanright?

LESTER: I mean I completely agree that it's wrong.

DICKY: You saying I'm wrong? Me?

DickytheBrickiethebestintheWestfuck'emandleave'em-
andshagalltherest? Wrong?

LESTER: Good God. Is that the time?

Dicky's missus took it all in good part, apologising for
being "a bit tipsy" as she paid us. The poor woman deserved
to be pissed as a newt. She reminded me of my mum who
endured similar social humiliation for many years when my
dad was roaming around as an undiagnosed schizophrenic.
Beer would bring out the worst in him too.

October 29th

Good old Tom Sangster. Yet again our Derek (recently
deceased) Guyler sound-a-like has pulled off another successful promotion at the Avon Rubber Social Club in Melk-
sham, Wilts. The Rubber Club as we call it, gives John
plenty of ammunition for the blunderbuss of rubber fetish
jokes he fires off throughout the night. An audience of tyre
manufacturers laugh as if they could never have imagined
such perversions in association with their industry. I dare say
the daily intake of toxic fumes severely affects the memory.

Anne and Taff's missus Claudia decide to catch the act for
the umpteenth time tonight. They are full of excitement and
almost irritating enthusiasm for their forthcoming ABBA
tribute. I suppose we were enthusiastic once. Laying awake
last night wondering what time Thomas would decide to
come home, I hit upon a possible name for the new venture. Having discarded "ABBA Gavenny" and Rob's tasteless
"ABBA Fan" (You may need to be Welsh to get the associations), I suddenly hit upon "ABBAriginal". This seems to go
down well. Well, better than "FLABBA" anyway.

The Idiot's Guide... No: 10
Come Together

"Come Together" was added to the Dart Board Band's set when we belatedly recognised that there was nothing from *Abbey Road* in the act. Having begun our time as bastard Beatles by recreating much of the psychedelic period, we extended the set to include many of the early songs. It seems odd now to think that at one time we did a rocking version of "Lovely Rita" but did not include "She Loves You" or "Please Please Me" in the performance. While we would always avoid the predictable, chronological "story of The Beatles" set, there is a subconscious obligation to present every period of The Beatles work.

Abbey Road is now well represented with "Here Comes the Sun" and the "Golden Slumbers" finale extending our range. "Come Together" usually goes down well at weddings given an introduction like: "And this is something the bride and groom hope to be doing later on..." Infact I sometimes wonder if we just select songs to impose our cabaret-style stand-up comedy on unwitting audiences.

"Come Together" was recognised by Chuck Berry as being a rewrite of "You Can't Catch Me" and as with "Surfin' USA" he has been rightly recompensed. John Lennon once said that if they hadn't invented the name rock'n'roll they would have called it "Chuck Berry". He covered "You Can't Catch Me" on his solo *Rock'n'Roll* album and remained one of the great interpreters of Berry's formula of a rhythm'n'blues riff fused with an up-tempo country shuffle, to create a sound which unified the music of black and white audiences.

"Come Together" however, is no straight twelve bar, three chord trick. It is even simpler, dwelling on the opening chugging riff in D for four bars with the words chanted over. What distinguishes the song is the "shhoooop" sound followed by McCartney's melodic bass pattern which hooks the listener as the drums roll around the kit with a subtlety not usually expected in an orthodox rock rhythm.

The lyric is in "Walrus" stream of consciousness style and so the lack of logic often causes me to forget the order of the verses and muddle the lines. Poor old John Freeman, singing the harmony parts, has been tempted to enrol in a course of extra sensory perception just to anticipate which line I'm about sing. Of course, we have the perfect get out. If anyone ever spots a mistake we simply pass it off as the "*Anthology* version".

The Beatles' *Anthology* albums have done a great deal to clutter the memory of the definitive recordings for me and I suspect, many other Beatles fans. In some ways the *Anthology* series works in the favour of tribute bands because it shows The Beatles with all their imperfections and inaccuracies and presents some songs in simplified, stripped down versions such as you might hear from a Beatles tribute too cheap to use a "keyboardmeister" like Rob Waller. You have been warned...

November

November 7th

Last night erstwhile drummer Tony Stockley set us up with a cabaret-type gig at his local, The Railway Inn in Westbury. Of course Tony wanted the gig in return for his labours which was fair enough, though Stuart is entitled to feel a little aggrieved at the prospect. There has been much swivelling of the drum stool between the two in recent months. With Taff occasionally engaged with Planet Janet and Tony drumming in just about every pit band in Wessex there inevitably has to be some flexibility.

Westbury defies all known principles of urban development. Despite claiming one of the most important railway junctions intersecting both Bristol and Plymouth lines to London, Westbury has remained uniquely under-developed. The famous chalk white horse on the downs overlooking the town, chokes and splutters behind the dusty clouds emitted by the nearby cement works. Little else threatens to mask the view of the horse from Westbury which seems trapped in a Victorian time warp of ruddy-bricked terrace houses and little, unprepossessing shops.

The "Sixties Night" cabaret takes place in the recently refurbished function room of the pub. All eighty or so tickets have been sold to an audience who are dressed as if they are going to the *Talk of the Town* which in Westbury terms, I suppose they are. The atmosphere is so dense with cigarette smoke, it appears that the pollution emitted by the cement works has taken an unexpected detour. We have agreed to play our extra rock covers set at the start and announce ourselves as the support band by the name of "Plus Support." The audience is neither amused, fooled nor impressed, knowing all too well that you don't get two bands for the price of one in Westbury.

Between the first set and Sgt Pepper, a comedian bridges the gap with an act well-honed in the social clubs of the South West. He is tall and mild mannered, looking like an Insurance Broker or Mortgage Consultant. On stage he tells decent jokes well but would hardly qualify for the alternative comedy circuit. This kind of audience still finds "Paki-gags" funny but don't expect to hear the word "fuck" mentioned on a night out. Not by the "turn" anyway. I see John wincing at the politically incorrect material but the lavatory humour goes down a bomb... so to speak.

We give a good account of ourselves and many of the audience hang around for a chat. One young woman, out with a husband who looks old enough to be her father, is heavily pre-occupied with my off stage persona, preferring me she says "in the wig and moustache." Several times she stumbles drunkenly through her fetish "for men with long hair" much to the chagrin of her balding husband. She demands I sign a band photo that she might keep at her bedside and observe while she and the old man are "'aving a girt bang." By now I am somewhat embarrassed for her husband who ushers her into a taxi whilst she promises him a "a girt wig for Christmas." There is something decidedly unflattering about all this. It would be nice, for once to be adored when the wig comes off. Never mind. I should be grateful at my age I suppose, to be in possession of my own teeth.

November 9th

Postscript to Saturday evening: With the gig just up the road from his house, Tony decided beforehand to leave his car and drums in the pub car park. Having downed a few pints during the course of the evening, he then decides to risk driving 200 yards back to save time in the morning. Sadly, on his way out of the car park he fails to see a low wall and carves a huge indentation in the car door. The local garage claim his luck is in as they have just acquired a similar car for scrap and can swap the doors. As it happens they are wrong. The recycled doors don't fit. Tony's car is then left in the garage overnight without doors with the consequence of leaving the interior light on and running down the battery which, in turn, screws up all the digital electronic programming. Reminiscences of crashing his hired camper at Glastonbury come hurtling to mind. If Tony added up all his earnings from Sgt Pepper over the last few years, it might just about cover his garage bills.

November 16th

My proposal to Millfield's Director of Music that we perform a joint concert with the choir has been leapt upon by the Headmaster, the Bursar and the new Marketing Department. Despite my efforts not to overstate my own increasing commitments to the Dart Board Band, they seem only too keen to be involved. Millfield is a good at encouraging staff and pupils to extend their talents, even it seems, in the lurid world of the tribute business. The charity concert on the weekend before the 60th anniversary of Lennon's birth next year has been agreed and accepted by the venue, St. John's, Smith Square.

St. John's is one of London's top classical music venues and naturally they have expressed some worries about noise levels. As they are basing their concerns on a previous concert by Suggs of Madness, I convince them that we are not in the same ear-bashing league as the "nutty boys".

In addition, I have received an encouraging response from Liverpool University Choir about a similar concert for December 9th, 2000, to mark the 20th anniversary of the great man's death. I have provisionally pencilled in St. George's Hall, Liverpool, a huge neo-classical edifice in the centre of the city. The costs are not insurmountable, giving us a reasonable chance to break even. If both these shows come off, I cannot help but think that we will be in the forefront of the Beatles tribute business.

This frightens me. In the past, whenever I've been about to set sail for a bright new horizon, be it in writing or performing, a stray torpedo has usually caught me across the bows and scuppered my hopes. *Waterloo Sunset* was the last of several sturdy vessels to go under. Afterwards I vowed never again to write a stage play. With the imminent publication of *An Audience with Ben Jonson* and Tony Barby's encouragement to work on a Beach Boys script, I'm beginning at last, to drift with the tide. Sgt Pepper is the one project I've really stuck with and our patience and adaptability have started to pay off. Despite this, I still can't quite believe that the route to future success will not be better charted behind a mine-sweeper.

November 25th

Three weeks of cancelled gigs and suddenly we're back in fashion. After taking yesterday off on the sick (only to feel decidedly better for a lie-in and an hour or two of tranquility), I return to work to receive a message on the voice mail from Dyrham Park, the National Trust stately home near Bath. Although their official who so enthused about us at The Bell earlier in the year had forgotten to pass on her recommendation, we have managed to wangle ourselves on the bill for next July's open air concert weekend. The Friday night will feature Jools Holland and his Rhythm and Blues Orchestra, whilst the Saturday goes distinctly more commercial with Voulez Vous the Abba tribute; something called Greased Lightening featuring Olivia Newton-John and John Travolta lookalikes; with ourselves as the opening act. I don't mind opening for Voulez Vous but Greased Lightening sounds cheesier than a night out in Cheddar. Still, with an anticipated audience of six thousand, we can't afford to be choosy.

November 29th

This evening I run into John at Frome College when picking up Richard from a school play rehearsal. He greets me with further good news that we're booked to play at the annual convention for the Licensers and Victuallers Association in Bath, next February. This has been booked on the recommendation of Roger following his daughter's wedding in Clearwell Castle. Although it comes the day before our proposed trip to Edinburgh, we can hardly afford to turn it down. Not that the fee is exceptional but the whole event will be nothing short of a huge audition before the assembled publicans and hoteliers of the West Country. With our recent ad in *The Stage* attracting some interest, we are gradually becoming less dependent on constant lobbying for gigs. In a month in which we have had three consecutive gigs cancelled, there is still a great deal to hope for.

The Idiot's Guide... No: 11
Golden Slumbers

Sgt Pepper's Only Dart Board Band had long wanted to try their luck by doing the entire second side of the *Abbey Road* album. The problem was that most of our gigs were private functions or pubs, where the public want to get up on their feet and remain there. When the opportunity came to plan for the choral events in concert halls we decided to include the last section of *Abbey Road*, beginning with the song "Golden Slumbers".

Abbey Road side two, is a landmark in rock music. The way the songs segue into one another suggests a concept of genius. Infact, as I understand it, Lennon and McCartney had a number of unfinished songs or musical sketches, all of which could not be included if developed. I have read that George Martin suggested that Paul join the songs together in a thematic, symphonic structure. George Martin was always finding ways of bringing his classical training into the Beatles sound. He was also able to realise sounds in the studio that only existed in John or Paul's head.

As a teacher, I can relate to what it must have been like dealing with the precocious, unorthodox talent of the Fab Four. Their individuality, immaturity and arrogance must have sometimes been exasperating but their talent was one to be nurtured. Martin's role was something of a balancing act, allowing their uninhibited, instinctive but often uninformed musical ideas to develop whilst subtly suggesting changes, additions and arrangements. Listen again to the atmospheric songs of The Kinks or the grandiose scale of The Who's *Tommy* and note how simplistic the arrangements are by comparison to The Beatles. Other bands of the late sixties were still singing "la, la, la" arrangements where The Beatles would be using strings or brass. Yet in "Lady Madonna" when they sing "pa, pa, pa" in the instrumental and under the final verse, it is stylistic and deliberate, avoiding the obvious brass overkill that might have been created. Similarly, on the "na, na, na" coda to "Hey Jude" the chorus of voices is contrasted by some powerful but subtle orchestral textures lower in the mix.

The Phil Spector production on the *Let It Be* album avoids delicate embellishments, leaving the melodic but plodding title track to the band's instinctive understanding of how best to "build" the song. When he does use orchestration and (much to The Beatles' consternation) choral voices on the "The Long and Winding Road" it has all the symphonic subtlety of a she-elephant in labour.

The spectre of Spector loomed large when thinking through choral arrangements. The last thing the Dart Board Band wanted was to sound like The Mike Samms Singers. We tried to ensure that there was no over-embellishment of "ooohs", "ahhs" and "laas" (as found in the standard choral arrangements) and instructed the choirs to be selective in their accompaniment and join with harmonies that were already in the recorded versions.

"Golden Slumbers" begins with McCartney delicately singing an apparent lullaby only to launch into the raucous chorus which anticipates the second verse which, in turn, leads into a reprise of the earlier song "Carry that Weight". This proves an ideal cue for a choir to enter, in full, football terrace mode. John and I then harmonise on the reprise of "You Never Give Me Your Money" that follows, which incorporates a string section. It is difficult for Rob Waller to maintain the piano part whilst playing synthesised strings simultaneously but he somehow manages and we launch back into the "Carry that Weight" chorus. The song then links into its finale with the "Oh yeah, alright" line a la McCartney, before giving Stuart Berry a rare opportunity in a Beatles set of playing a drum solo. The guitars crash in on the A7/ D7 riff that follows, Lester plays the solo note for note and John and I hit the falsetto "Love you" refrain. With a full choir in attendance this reaches a raunchy, gospel climax before suddenly stopping to allow the piano to hammer out the repeated chord into the final bars of "And in the End..."

Like much of the *Sgt Pepper* album, the end of *Abbey Road* is a glorious concept devoid of tangible narrative or meaning. It is held together by musical ingenuity, contrasting sophisticated arrangement with raw edged rock. It is a celebration of creativity and provides a fitting end to what was George Martin's final album with The Beatles.

December

December 3rd

Today I am forty three. The morning begins with the usual rush to hit the road to Street following the effluence-producing lorries and tractors that line the route. I have yet to learn why tractors find it necessary to appear on our roads at all, given that they are designed to travel across a field, which is surely the quickest way of getting anywhere in Somerset.

Arriving at Millfield, I am greeted by a complaining letter about my management of the theatre during the school play. I won't bore you with my defence but rest assured, I am suitably affronted. I threaten to resign as Theatre Manager. At least the issue may have drawn attention to the difficulties inherent in the job. Somehow I don't think I'm going to be allowed to throw in the towel that easily.

We are playing at another of Bradford on Avon's pub music venues, The Bear. An evening with the band seemed to be the best way to forget about clocking up another year. When Taff rings at 5.30 however, I begin to doubt the wisdom of working through a birthday. Taff is in his car, heading for Bath where he intends to catch the early show at the Theatre Royal. He is just checking to make sure we haven't got a gig. His mum had seen a poster in Bradford but he knew nothing of the event and assumed Tony was drumming. This booking came through John and so I have no idea who is to blame. Tony is unavailable and with no other real alternatives, we are forced to fall on Taff's sense of duty. He duly turns the car round and heads back home to collect his kit. We agree to refund the forty quid he has lost. This sum exceeds the fee any of us will receive for the performance.

As it happens, The pub fills up, the gig goes well despite the unforced three-week break. Tonight all those old jokes about being the only Beatles tribute older than the originals are recited on my part with some pathos.

December 4th

Planet Janet's Christmas bash at the Frome Rugby Club. Taff's drumming is comparatively sedate and the rest of the backing band shrink into the shadows of the backdrop as the three girls in impossibly high beehive wigs and Supremes-style costumes, take us through a funny and slick tour of the *Phil Spector Christmas Album* and much besides. Claudia, Taff's wife, has a great presence as the tall, central singer and I am confident that she and Anne will look well matched in their ABBA tribute roles next year. Amongst the audience is my old friend Mary Kirkman, a dynamic costume designer with a down to earth Mancunian sense of humour. Mary is small but terrier-like and can dominate conversations like no other. When a birthday parade is formed on the stage, I quietly point out to Mary my gratitude that Taff has a particularly bad memory and has overlooked that it was my birthday yesterday. This is a grave mistake. Mary immediately leaps from her seat and in front of over 200 people yells out like Vera Duckworth calling last orders at the Rovers Return: "'Ang on a minute! Oi! You lot! You've forgotten summat. It was Martin Dimery's birthday yesterday!" This resulted in me going on stage with three others to shake some sleigh bells to the tune of "Happy Birthday" which is of course, owned by Paul McCartney. Somehow I never quite seem to get a night off.

After the show Mary and her husband Chris come back to the house. Mary and I have shared many past pleasures as director and designer, most notably during my spell at the Theatre Royal Bath as Youth Theatre Director. It was only a part-time attachment which had to sit alongside my commitments to Frome College and the Merlin Theatre. During this period of overwork I desperately needed the support of Mary who always came up with superb results on a shoe-string budget. Having lost contact in the last year it was good to talk but the occasion was made more poignant in that Mary has suffered a relapse of the cancer that she seemed to have kicked five years ago. Despite her condition, Mary and I inevitably end the night in heated discussion. It's nearly always the same. We both drink too much and she drags up some old grudge which finds me running through self-justifications like a man in the dock. Mary is not one to let a sleeping dog lie. In fact she takes great pleasure in waking it up with a sharp stick and waving a raw steak under its drooling jaws. Thank God she still has the strength and will-power to give me a hard time. When an evening with Mary ends in harmony and tranquility, I will start to worry for her.

December 10th

End of term. The last term of the decade, century, millennium, etc: Normally I'd be doing a turn in the staff party. I'm beginning to run out of George Formby songs to corrupt in a crude attempt at in-house humour and so am only too pleased to leave the ukelele banjo in the cupboard this year.

Actually, the staff room is always over-crowded and with so many talented ego-maniacs on the staff, I doubt that my presence will be missed from a bill which is annually becoming longer than the *Royal Variety Show*. Ironically, I'm rushing away from Millfield in nothing short of contemptible haste to get on the road to Oxford, where I'm actually being paid to entertain at another public school.

The pupils of St. Edward's School in Oxford are not allowed home until Saturday morning, which makes the last Friday night of term one of high amusement for the kids and a nightmare for the staff. So as to take pupils' minds off pillow fights and inflating condoms with gas from the chemistry lab, a bunch of lackeys called Sgt Pepper's Only Dart Board Band have been booked to help pass the evening in a more passive manner. The New Hall at St. Edward's is one of the best concert venues in the city and tonight holds the entire school of 600 plus staff. The noise in the auditorium reverberates backstage and is reminiscent of the excitement that occurred at Millfield on Monday.

In an attempt to do something different for the day pupils, other than the tedious House dinner, I arrange a dance in the theatre with Studio 54, a seventies disco/ boogie band featuring Tony Barby, Louise and Marina from *Waterloo Sunset* as part of an eight piece line-up. By the end of the evening, pupils are almost hanging off the gallery in attempts at dance floor showmanship to the persuasive beat of "Hot Stuff".

It was reassuring to note that most public school kids are the same. Every hour of every day is organised for them. They are given limited freedom to get kicked out of pubs, fight in discos or even be part of the character-building, Saturday-job, child-exploitation racket. The pot of frustration is always simmering away and at social occasions the lid literally blows. State school kids usually need winning over. They need coaxing out of their inhibitions and are less easily impressed. Within twenty minutes of starting at St. Edward's, anxious teachers are clearing chairs from the auditorium to prevent serious accidents as the entire school flocks towards the stage. Individuals clamber onto the apron, others body-surf over the heads of the audience and total anarchy is threatened. I permit myself a wry grin as I watch teachers launch themselves into the fray to stop the surfers falling headfirst onto the floor and to tear apart snogging couples. That was my role on Monday, preventing anarchy. Tonight I am helping to cause it.

Meanwhile, at The Cheese and Grain Hall, Anne looks on in apprehension as a tall, leather clad Mohican invades the stage during Neon Monkey's set and, elbowing young Richard to one side, decides to take the lead vocals to Green Day's "Basket Case". As the boys are playing "Hitchin' a Ride" at the time, the effect is less than complementary. Fortunately he falls off the stage in a fit of ecstasy (in both respects) having already hurtled into a lighting stand and caused the biggest firework display this side of the Millennium. Anne's initial response is, "Thank God Martin's not here or there'd be a fight." Having now seen the video of the event, if she thinks I would have taken on a shaven headed, six-foot-five punk rocker with tattoos on his tongue, then she obviously regards my sanity with some suspicion.

On this occasion Neon Monkey play support to local luminaries Far Cue – a splendidly subtle name for a punk band. The boys account well for themselves before a big audience and are not phased by the nutters on the dance floor. For all the anarchy in our audience, we were certainly in a safer, better organised environment than at the Cheese and Grain.

Playing their kind of music, Neon Monkey face audiences not unlike those we used to encounter with Who Two. At Biker Conventions and the like, you are learning to survive on stage in a way that cannot be compared with the conventional theatre audience. When actors talk on TV chat shows about stage fright and handling the audience, I feel like writing in to tell them to try playing on a stage of wooden planks supported by beer crates in front of a bunch of drunken football hooligans at the Monkey Club, Swindon.

Now *that's* an adrenaline rush. Of course, no one summarised this better than Pete Townshend himself in the song "Long Live Rock":

> *"The place was really jumping to the Hi-Watt amps*
> *When a twenty inch cymbal fell and cut the lamps.*
> *In the blackout they dance right into the aisles,*
> *And as the doors fly open even the promoter smiles!*
> *Someone takes his pants off and the rafters knock-*
> *Rock is dead they say... Long live rock!"*

December 19th

After Thursday's seasonal return to The Riverside at Bradford, we are back at The Bell in Bath for a Sunday lunchtime Christmas special.

I awake feeling as if a pneumatic drill has been pummelling at my skull during the night. I've inevitably picked up the virus that has kept Anne off work for three days. Fortunately, I don't seem to have acquired the complementary sore throat. The phone rings; it's John:

"Alo odd boy (sniff), t's me. I'b peeling ter'ble. Bloody flu. Headache, sore throat, the lot." We quickly swap symptoms. He sounds worse than me but we'll both give it a go. There is one further problem: yesterday's heavy snow has not, as the weather people said, melted overnight. In fact it has formed the kind of surface nobody except Torville and Dean might find attractive.

Rob phones. He is angling none too subtly for a cancellation, "what with the weather and you two feeling so bad." I suspect he may have a conflict of interests.

An hour later Rob arrives at my house to warn us that, "according to Teletext, a lorry has jack-knifed at Limpley Stoke." We decide to take an alternative route into Bath. Twenty minutes and several near misses later, we realise that the main road was indeed the best bet and re-route. Rob stops along the way to talk to an old secretary of his who has pulled into the roadside. John and I and about twenty other cars make a peaceful train as she asks Rob's advice as to whether she should continue into Frome to collect her Christmas turkey or not. Rob is never one to be impolite and they remain chatting by the roadside whilst gridlock develops in their wake. Eventually after much wild gesticulation, Rob recommences the procession. Passing by the end of my road a mere thirty minutes after originally leaving the house, we seem at last, to be making some progress when Rob suddenly stops for petrol. John decides to continue and we both ponder Rob's characteristic lack of urgency. Once, during the middle of the second set with the audience up dancing and the adrenaline pumping away, we started counting in the next number to be interrupted by Rob declaring he wasn't ready. Assuming he was resetting his synthesiser, we held back for the customary five seconds. Still he wasn't ready. The entire band turned simultaneously to our left where we note that Robert is cutting his fingernails. "That one on the end's getting in my way," he helpfully demonstrated, holding aloft the offending digit. Given that I may be wrestling with the makings of a stomach ulcer, I can only admire such a sense of perspective.

As late as we are, it is for once, a relief to see Stuart's camper van just a few cars in front of us as we slowly trail into Bath. It is also a relief to see no jack-knifed lorry at Limpley Stoke.

With an in-house PA at The Bell, setting up is relatively quick and we begin on-time to a disappointingly small audience. Gradually though, the place fills with Christmas shoppers and Welsh refugees from the postponed Bath versus Swansea rugby tie. By the interval, the pub is so crowded we decide it's not worth queuing at the bar for a drink and after a token break, launch, at the request of a punter, into "I

Am the Walrus" in memory of his recently departed pal Irish Brian who appears to have been a bit of a folk-hero in Bath. Reportedly, his wake took in most of the city's hostelries.

With Irish Brian's mates now all rooting for us, the headaches and sore throats melt away more quickly than the snow outside and we are given another bone-shaking reception. At times like this as we bow, I look down at my feet, swollen and cripplingly encased in undersized Chelsea boots. I look down and just listen to the plaudits and think: Hang on to these moments. Enjoy the applause. Milk it. It can't last forever.

Of course, the applause is really for John, Paul, George and Ringo. I know that. I was rightly laughed at by my mate from work Dick Ransley, when I tried to explain our relationship with an audience. I said that when onstage I'm a medium through which the audience can relate to The Beatles. "Oh, I see," said Ransley. "You're rock'n'roll's answer to Doris Stokes." What I meant (as I tried in vain to explain to the giggling Ransley) was: The whole tribute band phenomenon is based on a massive suspension of disbelief, more than any other form of theatre. We know we are not The Beatles. The audience knows we are not The Beatles. But we pretend to be The Beatles and they pretend that we are The Beatles. This pact of self-deception becomes almost quasi-religious at times but no one is harmed. They go back to their Beatles albums and we go back to our day jobs.

I have come to accept that as a writer and performer that my own original work, whatever its merits, will never begin to achieve the epoch making acclaim of my heroes. Even if it did, how would I react to that success? Would I be able to comprehend and enjoy it the way I enjoy playing at John Lennon? What does it say about me that I feel more comfortable hiding behind a familiar wig, make-up and costume instead of going out there as myself? Did I ever really want success in my own right? If I cast my mind back to that little boy miming "She Loves You" with an air guitar to the crackly reproduction of my parents radiogram, I guess that all I ever wanted to be was a Beatle.

December 25th

With his partner away and the boys spending the morning with their mum, John gratefully spends Christmas Day with Anne and me. It is only the second Christmas Anne and I have spent at home in our married life. Olivia is disappointed at not sharing the excitement of Christmas morning with her cousins David and Ryan, but the rest of us relish the comfort and quiet of our own home. The day is pleasantly uneventful apart from Anne's car breaking down on the way back from giving the pony his seasonal feed. This matter was easily remedied with the help of jump leads but further confirmed Olivia's view that it was the "worst Christmas ever." This was despite being in receipt of two hundred quid's worth of new cymbals for her drum kit.

I break my acid-induced embargo on alcohol, and treat myself to a couple of glasses of Sainsbury's best with little discomfort. I have invented a new joke for the act at my own expense: "In the sixties we used to be on acid. Now we're on antacid. From LSD to Wind-eze." The audience at The Bell didn't laugh much either.

December 30th

After a fleeting visit to Luton we arrive at Hadham Hall in advance of the Millennium Eve celebrations. Paul Price has been in his element organising much of the event and takes great pride in his recently pirated CD collection that will bridge the gaps between our specially extended sets.

Whilst helping some of the residents carry equipment across to the huge marquee situated on their communal lawn, I am informed that George Harrison is in hospital following an attack on him at home by a crazed knife-wielding stalker. I am genuinely relieved to hear that he is recovering and not just because of the negative effect it might have on tomorrow's audience. It is at times like this one feels very grateful to be able to bask in The Beatles glory without actually being one.

December 31st 1999 to January 1st 2000

The balloons are inflated, the Roman Candles ready to ignite and the champagne corks about to burst. After a rushed and condensed Beatles set we exit to allow Pricey's impressive disco discs to dominate dance proceedings. A microphone crudely rigged to an old radio brings Hadham Hall, Hertfordshire, in touch with the rest of the planet. Earlier in the day we watched on TV as Auckland, Sydney and others exploded in an orgy of gunpowder and the new age swept in like a tidal wave from the East. Now it was our turn. I stood with Anne, she in her Abba wig and costume, me in the Lennon gear, both looking at a distance almost as we did twenty five years ago. Anne and Claudia are minutes away from making their Abbariginal debut and naturally more pre-occupied by that than anything else in the cosmos. Midnight strikes, the balloons cascade down (after a determined tug at the net) and all 250 party-goers spontaneously erupt. I seek out Richard and to his embarrassment give my "little" boy a very public hug and kiss. Eventually, Olivia emerges from the crowd and she too succumbs to her dad's emotional embrace. Twinges of regret cannot be hidden that Tom, our eldest, is 200 miles away sharing this moment in history with his girlfriend Willow and friends in Cardiff.

Rob reluctantly breaks from Tonya and takes the limelight to begin "Auld Lang Syne". We follow up with "All You Need is Love" reflecting events at the slightly more elaborate Dome down in Greenwich. Fortunately the audience join in with vigour, effectively disguising my emotionally trembly and quavering rendition.

John holds the audience for a minute while Lester swaps on to bass and I squeeze to the side of the tiny stage. On the count of four we begin the vamp the intro to "Waterloo" and the be-sequinned seventies duo Anne and Claudia skip onto the stage for their debut. They are well rehearsed compared to the band for whom this is most definitely a one-off performance. The girls (supported by Taff's very confident rhythm) sail through their five-song set with growing confidence and charisma and are immediately snapped up to play at the proposed summer ball.

Over the last few months of planning, Anne's enthusiasm for the project has become all-consuming. Now with their debut behind them just minutes into the new millennium, she looks as happy and proud as I've ever seen her. Why she gave up performing at the age of eighteen when singing so clearly courses through her veins, I will never know. Where I have always sought to widen my interests to the point of exhaustion, Anne seemed too readily to have settled for being either a bank clerk or a mother and failed to maintain any outside interests. In recent years horse riding has provided her with an occupation away from the home but I have a strong suspicion that Jake, our placid Welsh Cob, is about to go through a period of emotional neglect.

Anne's dad, musical veteran of so many New Year parties, listens to Anne's humble interpretation of her musical renaissance before retorting with: "Anne, you couldn't hit a bum note if you tried." Yet the last time she sang was probably when guesting for his trio a quarter of a century ago. As they say, once you've got it, you never lose it.

In 1978, three months after our marriage, Anne and I spent New Year's Eve in London where we lived. We were invited to a party by our old school friend Douglas McFerran. For many years Douglas and I were the closest of friends and at the same time, rivals. He often likened our respective career paths to Robert Frost's poem "The Road Not Taken". Douglas chose to be an actor, to never marry or have children and to devote his life to success in the theatre business. I took the other route, trying to achieve a stable marriage, having children, earning a regular income from teaching. I never gave up the idea of being a success as a writer or performer. Living so far from London and having others dependent on my income has perhaps prevented me from fully exploiting my opportunities as a teenage hopeful in the National Youth Theatre class of '73.

Doug has gone on to become a well-known face on television and the stage. He would have loved to have been our generation's great Hamlet or an Oscar winning film star. Those achievements have been soaked up by the likes of Kenneth Branagh and Daniel Day Lewis. The latter being an actor with whom we have both appeared in our early days. Doug and I see each other about once every five or six years with little contact in between. When we meet I enjoy his eccentric company immensely but cannot resist the temptation to impress upon him my less high profile achievements as if trying to justify the path I chose at the fork that separated us. For his part, I think Doug has withdrawn from confronting my domestic happiness so as not to serve as a reminder of the sacrifices he has also made.

That New Year of 1978 we made our way through the snow-bound streets of Holland Park to the plush apartment Doug shared with his girlfriend Sabrina. Sabrina was the daughter of an eminent Armenian artist whose paint-sculptures in mud had earned him international acclaim. The elegant flat was his base when he chose to visit Europe from his home in New York. The snow and a public holiday had returned the streets to the pedestrian and also to a semblance of their late Regency splendour.

On the first day of '79 we walked across to Kensington Gardens, reflecting the past decade and looking in anticipation towards the next. We then tried to envisage where we might be on New Year's Eve 1999. I had a vague notion of being with the usual revellers in Trafalgar Square but had held the view that a nuclear holocaust would see to us all before the turn of the century. Sabrina looked at me with a mixture of sadness and amusement. "Do you really believe that?" she said, half-hoping I was kidding. Douglas just thought I was a flimsy CND pacifist. Politics seemed to play such an important part in our lives then. The East-West polarities dominated our everyday thinking, our approach to life and our creativity. Virtually all my early plays had some kind of anti-war message.

The world map has changed more than anyone could have imagined. Neither could we have suspected that we were about to live out most of the century under the unbroken tenancy of successive Conservative governments. It would have been hard to imagine that the outgoing Labour government on the brink of the Winter of Discontent would suffer eighteen years of inner turmoil, moving further to the right than the embryonic SDP before returning to power.

It was not difficult to guess that Douglas, despite being expelled from Drama school, would eventually make it in the business. None of us could have predicted that poor Sabrina would be the only one not to see out the century. Just a few years later she died from a heart attack whilst still in her twenties. Although they were separated when her UK visa expired, Doug kept close contact with Sabrina in New York. If he was ever going to marry, then Sabrina was probably the only candidate for the job.

Anne and I certainly could not have imagined how radically our lives would change just months later when I accepted my first teaching post on the Isle of Wight. We had always envisaged ourselves however, moving to the West Country. It was on a residential school trip to Gloucestershire that we first fell in love, so settling in Somerset after four years on the Island was not so much of a surprise.

Once we had decided that the world might not end quite so abruptly, Anne gave up work to focus on raising a family. Years of material hardship followed as teacher's salaries fell way below the average and I began to invest far more into my outside interests, wondering if I really had taken the right path at the crossroads.

If I could have gazed into the icy waters of the Serpentine on New Year's Day 1979 and seen Anne and I dressed in sequins and silk about to perform a cabaret entertainment in a village just outside Bishop's Stortford, would I have been alarmed or reassured by the future? I suspect I would have been just short of suicidal. Yet the lasting pleasure and pride at being a member of Sgt Pepper's Only Dart Board Band has only been outstripped by the pleasures of parenthood and the pride of seeing my first play in publication. Nothing in my professional career has given me so much sustained amusement as being a poor man's Beatle.

Our year 2000 diary is already filling up with musical engagements. Some could prove to be the biggest, most highly publicised performances any of us will ever undertake. Some of those youthful ambitions of 1979 may yet be achieved in advancing middle age.

I am still treading that mysterious path to fulfilment. My path may not have been the most direct and there have been many fallen branches along the way. Of all possible paths however, it has been by far the most beautiful, scenic and diverting. May it never reach an end.

Martin Dimery. Jan 1st. 2000

Epilogue
Tomorrow Never Knows...

I suppose Sgt Pepper's Only Dart Board Band must have achieved something since I wrote this diary. We certainly seem to spend less time fighting with the audience and changing in storerooms and toilet cubicles – two signs of encroaching "respectability" I suppose. It doesn't mean gigs are any more memorable or amusing though. I think the diary is more typical of the struggling rock band than anything we've moved onto and is, as such, a better and more accurate description of the real world of live music. Another thing that has changed is our stage names. It was felt we needed to re-invent ourselves a little.

We now go under the nom-de-tribute of John Legend; Paul McCoatoff, Rolf Harrison, Gringo Barr and of course Sgt Pepper on keyboards. We've had name checks on BBC 1 and Radio 2, a fair bit of press here and there, so in theory, more people should have heard of us. But in all honesty, I doubt that the public remember the names of tribute bands anyway. One is much the same as any other. Tribute bands might give an increasing number of musicians a better living but this particular pact with the devil is unlikely to make many of us wealthy or famous.

Many of the plans illustrated in the diary have come to pass, others haven't. We were not (mercifully) flown to Edinburgh and back on a freezing February night. Neither did the Licensers and Victuallers' Ball prove to be an open cheque book. On the contrary, the evening consisted of trying to pacify some very drunk erstwhile barmaids and bouncers. Now you tell me, who do you turn to when an audience full of bouncers gets out of hand?

As suggested, the big Clark's do didn't happen but Abbariginal did. Infact, they got to be very good before disbanding somewhat prematurely due to conflicts of commitments. Anne has hopes of starting a new ABBA tribute as I write.

The really big events did, I am pleased to say, come to pass. The choral event at St. John's Smith Square proved a delightful evening although the venue was not the best in London for attracting a rock music audience. The Liverpool event with the choir of the University was switched to the Philharmonic Hall by the conductor Gareth Wall. It proved to be a great move.

These events and the wonderful tour of Germany and the Czech Republic are referred to in the letters that follow.

The biggest concert we have so far been engaged to deliver was at Dyrham Park, near Bath. Following Jools Holland's triumph the previous evening, we stepped out in front of some four thousand paying customers as the warm up act for the Abba tribute, Voulez Vous.

The sheer size of the stage as viewed on our arrival was enough to turn the bowels into custard. We got through the soundcheck, dinner and all the other formalities, by ironically complaining about everything:

"Hmmn, not sure about the sound system," said John.

Being John Lennon

"They should have got in the one we had at Coleford Village Fete last week."

"What, the one made up of stolen car stereo speakers?" retorted Lester, catching the train of thought.

"Don't like this food," said Rob.

"We expect a better pre-gig meal than this."

"Yes" replied Lester, "I still think about that bag of Porky Scratchings we had at the Hayloft in Radstock."

Naturally, being England in the peak of summer, it was raining. Looking out from the stage at the audience seated in the natural amphitheatre of the three surrounding steep hills, I could barely believe the people furthest away on the top of the incline opposite could actually hear us. I asked them to wave their umbrellas if they were listening. They did so. There followed the creation of a uniquely Anglo phenomenon: "The British Wave" in which thousands of colourful umbrellas moved up and down in sequence and in defiance against nature. There can be nothing more heartening than the British, in deck chairs, defying their miserable climate in the pursuit of happiness.

I think it's fair to say the adrenaline was coursing through our veins and we peaked well. The audience responded enthusiastically and we certainly warmed them up for a night of Abba kareoke courtesy of Voulez Vous with their splendid range of electronic equipment, guaranteed to ensure every show sounds the same. For us, however, the experience was truly unique, a one-off.

My close friend Mary Kirkman finally succumbed to cancer just over a year after the diary entry in which she features. Her husband Chris had the bright idea, in her final weeks, to instal e-mail to her bedside computer. Unable to always take calls or receive visitors, this was a splendid way of keeping Mary in touch with the world and I took advantage of the opportunity to catalogue, for her amusement and my own, the continuing story of Sgt Pepper's Only Dart Board Band:

E-mails to Mary

E mail no: 1

Dear Mary,

Chris told me that you were on-line and high tech. What a brilliant idea. I found e-mail really useful when organising our tour in the summer to Homberg and Prague. Avoiding phone conversations in broken English, German or Czech was a great luxury this time around.

The tour was brilliant. Christine set us up with two excellent gigs, one of which was at a medieval castle courtyard. The Czechs also did us proud. Abbariginal really came together well and were particularly good on the Czech leg of the tour. One night in the town Trhove Sviny (literally translated "Pigmarket") we played on the local outdoor ice hockey rink. Of course the lack of ice in summer negated the need to bring in Torville and Dean. Five hundred turned up and all three bands went down a storm. Infact, as I stood at the back of the arena keenly watching Neon Monkey (our lads' band) doing their twenty minute punk set, a lightning storm was breaking in the nearby border hills of Austria. Tom, Rich and Greg (John's son) stole the show that night. A predominantly young audience couldn't get enough of their Blink 182 and Green Day covers. Sgt Pepper's Old Farts Band were a bit of a come down afterwards. Claudia smugly wondered how I felt about being upstaged by my sons. Now you would know Mary, as I stood at the back of that arena watching those boys leaping aroung the big canopied stage, illuminated by red profiles and bolts of encroaching lightning, stirring up a sea of bobbing heads, it was all I could do to stop the make-up from running. I guess when Katrin starts doing these things, as she surely will, Claudia will know the feeling.

The tour ended with the Dart Board Band doing a show at this big nightclub on the riverbank in central Prague. It is impossible to get a coach to stop outside the venue due to tram lines, so we were forced to pay exorbitant fees to taxi drivers, only for them to drop us and all our equipment about 100 yards from the door. Despite being exhausted even before we went on, the Cavern-like atmosphere generated in the live music basement drew lots of punters from the three upstairs discos to check us out. By 1.00 am the place was heaving, mostly with tourists – and we played a blinder. Some lads from Liverpool actually came backstage afterwards asking which part of Merseyside we were from.

"A blinder" is not how I'd describe the way we played when challenged, in Germany, by a local football team. We conscripted a full squad with Marina Sossi (by no means the least talented of our defenders) accompanied at full back by Lester Mason, taking his first exercise in 15 years. Rob Waller's personal trainer Tonya, forbade him the chance to play on account of it "killing him." We embarked on our team bus at the hostel for the short journey into the nearby village of Schwarzenborn. Now as it turns out, Schwarzenborn is infact a city, the smallest in Germany. Schwarzenborn (or Blackburn City as the locals translated it) makes Wells look like New York. Their footballers also have pretentions to being the Teutonic version of Blackburn Rovers. Expecting a kick-about on the local park with a few coats as goal posts, we sought directions to the Sportsplatz. As the coach turned into the appointed road, a howl somewhere between desperation and laughter broke out. We were playing at the local football stadium. In the natural amphitheatre surrounded by advertisement hoardings and trainers' dug outs, the groundsman worked with the precision of an architect on cutting perfectly geometric circles in the Wembley-like turf.

Were it not for their immaculate shiny green and black football kit, our opposition would have resembled extras from the cast of *Deliverance*. Our host, Uschi Becker, actually described these woodland people as "how you say – hillybillies." Fortunately we were being pitched against the veterans and reserve team left-overs. Naturally, they beat us, but 5-2 was a respectable score with one or two outstanding performances of the kind of English grit for so long absent from our National game. Kevin Keegan would have been proud of us. He would also have learned a lot from our tactics too, I've no doubt. The Germans soon stopped patronising us with their gentle possession football, when, against the run of play, a slight mis-kick from Dimery (R), rolled fortuitously into the path of Dimery (T) who shaking off an attempt to wrench out his nose ring by a vicious Hun centre half, slipped the ball cleverly to the balding but graceful Dimery (M) who stuck out a toe, closed his eyes and hit the ball with all the force his crumbling body could muster. The ball trickled towards the goal. The keeper, stunned that so much effort could produce so little effect, dived towards the ball but only succeeded to palming it into his own net. Dimery (M) took off like Fabrizio Ravenelli, shirt over head, in an elaborate victory celebration which nearly resulted in his temporary removal from the pitch on a stretcher. Team members under the age of twelve had to be restrained from miming loop the loops with arms aloft whilst singing *The Dambusters* tune. We were on dangerous territory here. The Germans, typically, responded with a five-goal bombardment, having persuaded the referee to extend the game from 20 to 30 minutes each way. In the final minute however, the dam broke again as Dimery (T) dashingly sporting jeans hoisted to the lower buttocks and cut off at the calf, dribbled past two defenders in the box. One tugged unsportingly at his borrowed Schwarzenborn third team strip, whilst the other careered into him with all the subtlety of a Panzer division. The boy fell like a conscript on the fields of Flanders. The referee had no choice. Cunningly playing the sympathy card, veteran defender John Freeman appointed his son Guy (aged 9) to take the penalty. Surely even the Germans could not spoil this last minute attempt to regain English integrity. Indeed, the goalkeeper's dive in the wrong direction won him few Oscars and Guy duly "tucked it away" to complete the plucky performance. We sought consolation in the fact that with away goals counting double, the German team was left with a mountain to climb in the second leg. As they live on one, they were unlikely to find this daunting. Our resolute if rag-arsed army enjoyed a drink with our hosts in Der Klubhaus and shared recollections of the appalling film *Escape to Victory* which we suddenly held in close affection.

To bring us firmly back down to earth, the next Dart Board gig after the "European Tour" was the West Wilts Dog Show. John still holds dear the stolen 11th place rosette found in the portakabin changing rooms. We've also done a show in London at the classical venue, St. John's, Smith Square for Lennon's 60th birthday. The Millfield Chamber Choir became our backing band for that one and the sound was lovely. I'll get you a CD of it as soon as they're finished. It wasn't a big turn out though, which leaves us worrying about our forthcoming gig at the Liverpool Philharmonic Hall on December 10th. Hopefully the University Choir will help us sell a few tickets. All proceeds from our choral ventures will go to charity, so we're feeling quite pious and deserving.

Anne is well but Abbariginal has stalled a bit with Lee's wife Tracey about to sprog and the keyboard player displaying all the tantrums of Elton John coming down off Prozac. At the last rehearsal, he had officially left. As they managed on the tour with all his parts mimed on click-track, this is hardly a bitter blow.

The kids are doing alright. Tom's now at Bath College on the BTEC course in Popular Music and finding the module on "Stage Posturing" much to his pleasure. Richard's about to do GCSEs and we are deliberately stunting Olivia's growth so that she remains our sweet, little girl.

I was pleased to see Ellen recently. She'll be big in TV I know... and not because of her uncle either.* I hope Sally and Tina are well too.

Obviously, the e-mail gives you the chance to communicate when you feel like it. Whenever you want a proper chat give us a call and I'll be round. Unless you find me, like many others, far more palatable by e-mail!

Loads and loads of love,

Martin.

N.B. * Ellen Kirkman launched a successful career at the BBC some time before her uncle, Greg Dyke, took over as Director General. Of course, although Ellen would not wish to take advantage, to my shame, I once attempted to exploit this tenuous connection. Mr. Dyke is obviously a man of greater integrity than I suspected.

E-mail no: 2

Dear Mary Dot Kirkman (As you are now apparently known),

Martin Dot Dimery here again. Thanks for your reply. I thought you might find some amusement in one or two anecdotes.

Well... what's new? Oh yes. It was my birthday Sunday. And no, I wasn't expecting you to remember. I'm 44. (Deep sigh followed by pathetic smile of passive acceptance). I've still got that wonderful waistcoat you made me when I was about 34. I managed to lean against some wet paint in the old Theatre Royal studio and got a bit of a black mark on the back, so it has to be worn with a jacket. But it still *is* worn. Mind you, I'm still wearing some ghastly old suits too, so that may not appear too much of a compliment. I've grown out of the TFJ's though. Remember them? The "Tight Fuckin' Jeans" rightly satirised by your Ellen. The waistcoat however, apart from the little black blob, is a classic. If I'd known then what I know now, I would have sued those buggers at the Theatre Royal Bath for an entire wardrobe.

Funny birthday. Woke up in a hotel room in Maidstone. No, I hadn't drunkenly got onto the last train out of Westbury by mistake. I was doing *On the Road* with City Lights. Remember that show? Maybe you've not seen it. It's the recital programme about Kerouac, Ken Kesey and that lot of old pre-hippy reprobates. It's a show that we hadn't done for over two years when suddenly, this Autumn, three bookings come in. All at inconvenient times. The last one was at Petersfield and the previous one, in October, came three days after the Sgt Pepper London gig and required driving on a Tuesday afternoon to Tunbridge Wells. Having then done a cabaret style floor show reading poems and singing hobo songs to the background of well heeled literati squeakily scraping their plates of Coq au Vin, I had to drive back in those torrential floods that were just beginning in Kent. Driving past the M25 turn off to Gatwick Airport with the radio telling me that it had closed due to the weather, was no great confidence booster for the rest of the journey. Naturally enough, it was up early to work the next morning and I capped the day off running around unconvincingly refereeing a school football match in conditions that can only be described as sadistic.

City Lights is an odd set up. Six performers (two musicians, three readers and me doing a bit of both), black folders, easy chairs and (apart from the long drive) an easy night's work. Sometimes we've played in very classy venues. On Saturday we were in a municipal-style hall which was an annex of a suburban library in Rochester. Twenty people turned up, most of whom looked as if they had expected a bingo night. Still, a hundred quid and an en-suite hotel room courtesy of the Arts Council, made the ignominy endurable. Of course, I missed Chilcompton's night of this or any year... Abbariginal... in person! By the sound of it, it was a bit more lively than the City Lights show. Packed beyond any sane fire regulations from what I hear. Anne seemed chuffed anyway. Her dad was there, which would have pleased her.

Next up, Liverpool. At last, those cod Scouse accents are going to be put to the test. Sunday is the big day. The University Choir are rehearsed and the 10 foot poster is being hoisted up on the Philharmonic Hall tomorrow. I'm already nervous and praying this fucking cold clears up in time, especially as we're recording it. Actually, before I get too carried away, the ticket sales need to pick up a bit. The hall holds 1700. At the moment we're hoping for at least 300 squeezed in the front seats downstairs to create a bit of atmosphere. It will need the University students to turn out on the night to get us even that many. You really need big money to promote these kind of gigs. It's something we're rather short of. Our man on the ground has been doing a good job with little cash and we just hope it pays off. We've really decided we don't want to play week-in week-out at Brannigan's Wine Bars. We want to do more big halls and theatres but without a big name promoter it's very hard.

Anyway, at some point I must tell you about our night in the monastery in the Czech Republic. It's worth saving until next time. I'll write again after Liverpool.

Lorra, lorra love,

Martin.

E-mail no: 3

Dear Mary Dot Kirkman,

Received your Christmas card this morning. Many thanks. I posted yours yesterday so it should arrive by January 22nd.

Well, I said I'd write to update you on the Further Adventures of the World's Oldest Beatles Tribute in the hope that you don't mind being the recipient of my therapeutic outpourings.

Liverpool... When I was a boy (in the early part of the last century) I always thought of Liverpool as a bleak, hard, rugged place full of meat-cleaver carrying dockers with forearms solid as an elephant's testicle. Now that the docks have become museums and bistros, the place more resembles Paris. Anne and I decided to make a weekend of it and stayed at an upmarket hotel overlooking the magnificent St. George's Hall. My God, the place is like the Parthenon. Some of the other Victorian buildings amazed me in their opulence. We never had anything like that in Luton. But then we never built a reputation on trading tobacco and slaves. In fact, since Liverpool and Bristol stopped exporting human beings to the colonies, Luton seems to have been receiving them back. Luton's traditionally been a good place to find employment but I've just heard on the news that the Vauxhall car plant is closing down. Luton *is* Vauxhall. They've been making cars there for 95 years. My old man spent 30 miserable years inside that factory. My father-in-law the same. To my mum's father, Vauxhall was a refuge from Folkestone in the thirties depression. He started on the production line and rose up to the dizzy heights of management. That was when they employed over 20,000 people. Still, I see they're keeping the Ellesmere Port plant open, giving Merseyside even more to crow about... but I digress...

Liverpool... In short, I loved it. We went up Mathew Street to see the shopping mall where the Cavern once stood. Then we went to the place they call the Cavern but isn't. Still, it gives you a fair impression of the original. It's so far underground. To think the whole of that street was like a massive underground warehouse for imports. I wasn't too impressed with the dodgy Beatles statues littering the place up. They looked less like the Fab Four than we do. On the Saturday night the University Choir and Orchestras were performing Mozart's Requiem at St. George's Hall, to which we were invited. Unfortunately they'd forgotten to put comps on the door but it was well worth the entrance. Actually, I'd booked St. George's for us that evening but I can see now why the University people wanted to swap us for the Philharmonic. St. George's is far too ornate for rock music. The sound would resonate too much.

The following day we met the Gareth (the student organising the Sgt Pepper event) outside the Philharmonic Hall. To his dismay, he discovered that the ten-foot poster that cost us 150 quid had been stolen from under the vandalised case outside the hall. Muttering something about insurance, we then proceeded to a rehearsal room in the University around the corner. From the size of the room it was clear that we weren't expecting the 70-strong choir of the previous evening. In fact we were down to 28 souls willing to put themselves out for John Lennon's 20th Anniversary. Judging from some of the desperate last minute photocopying going on, it was clear that many hadn't a clue what they were supposed to be singing. We soon realised that we were going to have to be on form and not depend on the enhanced choral sound too much. In London, the Millfield Choir did a tremendous job, not only singing but clapping and dancing like a gospel choir. But then, we'd rehearsed with them a few times. We thought that an older, bigger choir would be amazing and so we had to adjust our expectations somewhat.

The hall itself is pretty daunting. I don't think I've ever seen such a huge balcony, not from a stage anyway. Fortunately, we were closing the circle off and performing to the stalls only. This made it seem like a slightly more intimate venue. In all, the audience reached nearly 300, which isn't at all bad considering The Bootlegs were on in Liverpool the week before. This created the impression of a fairly full auditorium. We were preceded by the University Big Band so there were about 60 students involved altogether. Obviously none of them had many friends otherwise we might have filled the stalls comfortably. They did a fairly good half-hour before the interval, then it was our turn... 90-minutes straight through. We brought our soundmen, Richard and Q up from Wiltshire in their "Fresh Market Supplies" van. Richard and Q started doing sound for us at Clive Westmacott's Dickstock parties and are bloody good. Infact, Clive and Jo came all the way up to see us. We weren't informed in advance so you can imagine the look of surprise on Taff and Claud's face when, whilst waiting for the lift at their hotel, the doors open and there stands "Girt Shovel Hands Clive" like a walking spectre!

The get-in was complicated by an afternoon matinee needing to get out first. With only two-and-a-half hours to rig, Richard and Q were really pushed and having the Big Band onstage as well didn't help. Everything was going fine until the string sextet turned up and explained that they were, in fact accompanying us. This was the first we'd heard of it. A spare mike was found and after a lightning sound check with the string section, the audience were clamouring to be let in.

I'm pleased to say we played very well. My brother-law

Paul, came along and (having seen us more than most) actually thought the sound was the best he'd heard. The acoustic in the hall was brilliant. The choir was actually very good on most numbers. Trained musicians you see. The strings sounded great on "Yesterday" but couldn't be heard on the louder stuff. Still, they filled a gap on that enormous stage and looked good. The audience were a bit slow to respond at first. Perhaps they were expecting a more reverential occasion. "A Day in the Life" seemed to get them going though and by half way through they were clapping along and joining in. Most of them were up dancing by the end. It was very gratifying to go down well in the one place where you might expect people to be sceptical about Beatles tributes. What was also nice was what the heavily Scouse usher described as "shit loads of people" waiting to catch us after the show. My mum and her sister were there; Clive and Jo; my brother-in-law; his mate from Liverpool and his mate's entire family, plus good old George Williams*. George has now left Liverpool Institute of Performing Arts and seems to be heading more in the direction of music than acting. He was in fine form, upstaging us with his story of being personally tutored by McCartney on song writing. Bloody Hell! I'm glad he didn't bring Macca to the gig.

The next day Anne, Richard, Olivia and I (Tom being too "grown up" to attend these things) left Liverpool via a quick trip to Penny Lane. We didn't actually see any road signs. I suppose they keep getting nicked. Still, the shelter in the middle of the roundabout is still there but I'm not sure if the banker is still waiting for a trim. Driving on a little further, we came upon Menlove Avenue and stopped the car at number 251 where Lennon grew up. A single rose hung from the gate. It was all so unprepossessing despite the blue commemorative plaque which was only unveiled on Friday.

We moved on quickly. The current occupants must get fed up with people peering through their front window.

Now we're back and I'm on holiday... (yes...yes...I know... "you teachers in public schools... blah, blah, etc. etc.") I reckon I've earned the holiday this term. Things have been mad at Millfield since September but I won't bore you with the details. Except you may have seen in the papers (or perhaps you missed *The Sun* "exclusive") yet more scandal has hit the school. Two boys had a fight in the playground! (Gasp!) Yes! A proper fight! At Millfield! Where they pay lots of money to send their children! The school has been rocked again by controversy! Of course the fact that one of the boys was James Bond's son (Sean Brosnan) who was subsequently suspended, seems to be of interest. Funny thing is, Sean's in my media studies group and just before term ended we were studying the module: "Celebrity and the Tabloid Press." So now he knows. I bet he really suffered being suspended and having to skulk off back to his Malibu beachfront mansion two days early. And to think... he missed freezing his bollocks off in the Christmas carol service at Wells Cathedral. Ha! That'll teach him to fight in the playground!

Anyway, that's enough for now. I'm at home so if you feel up to it, get in touch. I still haven't told you about our night in the Czech monastery but it'll keep. I like to leave a cliffhanger ending in my e-mails. Actually, these communications are getting more like a soap opera. Is this the world's first e-mail soap? Send my love to Chris and the kids.

Lorra, lorra love, chuck,

Martin

---

*George was "Tommy" in our 1992 ECOS production. Pete Townshend's daughter Emma saw the show and was so impressed, she got George an audition in front of her old man for the West End production. Apparently the boy came close. A name to watch.

E-mail no: 4

Dear Mary (and whoever may chance to read this instalment),

As promised... the next episode of the e-mail soap, whether you like it or not.

Episode 4: The Monastery. (Dramatic Music over: Dum, dum duuuuum...)

On August 22nd we travelled down from Budejovice to the tourist town of Ceske Krumlov. Krumlov is breathtaking. One enters the town through massive arches that straddle a high opening in a cliff. The arches support a large section of the medieval castle. Once inside the gateway you cross a bridge over the River Vlatava which also flows through Prague. The river curves in an almost circular bend which effectively creates a natural moat around the inner town. Having fallen into various passing hands over the centuries, Krumlov reflects many different eras. The most striking architecture is the Baroque which, since the fall of Communism, has been restored superbly throughout the country. The Czech Republic is justifiably pulling a lot of tourists north from Austria.

After doing the sightseeing bit, we then took the coach across the hilly terrain to the town of Nove Hrady (or Newcastle to you), where we were due to spend the night. Nove Hrady sits on a high tor, its castle looking down forbiddingly on the surrounding fields and meadows. The castle gleamed in the shafts of sunlight that had broken from the backdrop of menacing, almost brown thunderclouds gathering to the south over in Austria. It was eerily reminiscent of the carriage approach to the Castle Dracula in a Hammer Horror. Navigating the windy roads with extensive wear on its gearbox, the bus finally arrived at the little town square. Just off the square stood the medieval monastery.

What surprised us was how new the place looked. It wasn't in the least dreary and depressing. The stonework shone and was uncorrupted by pollution, unlike older English buildings. It transpires that the monastery had been taken over by the Communists and (surprise, surprise) turned into a military barracks. With the Austrian border only a short walk away, it is easy to see why. Left to total neglect by the authorities, the building was reclaimed and restored by the church in the last few years. Only three monks live at Nove Hrady and so its greater use seems to be as a hostel.

The only problem was that most of the party was to be accommodated in a new annex which effectively was a dormitory arrangement. Eight beds upstairs and eight down. Marina and Neil kindly offered to act as prefects in the upper dorm with all the kids. This noble gesture was soon rumbled when the rest of us recognised that our own dorm was, if not full of kids, certainly the more juvenile.

Returning after midnight from the wonderful gig at nearby Pigmarket Town Ice Hockey Arena, we unlocked the wrought iron gates to the monastery and with token attempts not to wake fellow residents, we piled into the dorm pathetically trying to conceal clanking crates of Budvar purchased from the local supermarket at 15p a bottle. Once inside our dorm we attempted to settle into our clean but unaired beds. The damp mattresses we were assured, were caused by a lack of recent use, rather than, as we expected, a visiting party from the Urinary Infections Wing of the local clinic. Lester Mason elected himself Head Boy and proceeded to make a speech of some significance:

"Now before we settle in for the night," he declared, pacing the room and gesticulating firmly with the neck of his bottle. "Before we settle in for the night, I'd like to get a few things straight. A few rules and regulations that I think might come in useful." John, myself, Nick (Marina and Neil's mate) and Pete the coach driver, had already started giggling in anticipation. Anne, Ros and Julie (Nick's partner) were, like the sensible girls they are, making serious attempts at applying cold cream and skin cleanser or delicately changing under the sheets.

"First of all," said Lester, his voice rising with authority, "First of all... no bed hopping after lights out. I don't want to be woken in the early hours of the morning by a cacophony of stifled grunts, thank you very much. Secondly... and this applies strictly to the boys... no making tents in the bed. Other people have to use them after you. Thirdly... and by no means less significant... no blowing off. And that includes you Rosalind." Ros responds by raising her eyes towards Anne in a "men never grow up, do they?" fashion. "We're all in this together," continues Lester, "and as far as I'm concerned, standards have to be maintained. Anyone caught breaching the rules will be sent immediately to Brother Dominic for a good seeing to. And we all know what that entails."

At this point, fuelled by a bottle too many of Budvar, a member (who shall remain anonymous for the sake of his shame... and no, it wasn't me) laughs so loudly he farts twice in the general direction of Ros whose look of mild amusement turns to one of alarm. Sensing she is about to bed hop to evacuation, I quickly chip in with "Er... Head Boy sir, I think two of your rules have already been flouted sir!"

Lester makes a half-hearted attempt at admonishing the offender before slumping onto his moist mattress and continues with a series of comic observations. Most are funny in their own right but being primed by Lester's own Tommy Cooper-type laugh, we start to get hysterical. Of course, I mean the boys in the room, all of whom are propped up in a row of beds, swigging back the Budvar. The girls are by now tutting and sighing in a desperate attempt to get us to shut up. By about 3 a.m. I am greatly relieved to be in the annex where we are less likely to cause disruption to the other fellow inmates. Even so, at any moment I am half-expecting a cowled figure with an oil lamp to come knocking angrily at the door.

The following morning we attend breakfast hoping to have got away with the raucous behaviour of the night before. No complaints have been lodged. Father Peter politely enquires as to the concert. He thinks we're an orchestra or something. We do nothing to change his perception. The breakfast is far better than we had been led to believe and sets us up for the three-hour journey to Prague.

Before leaving, whilst most make a final visit to the supermarket for further provisions, I slip into the monastery's church. The paintings, statues and plasterwork are all ornate and beautifully crafted. Although I find opulence and religion a difficult combination, I cannot help but marvel at the dedication given to this church and the heritage it leaves behind. Despite rather abusing the sanctity of the place the previous night, I am momentarily overcome by a great sense of peace and tranquility and can suddenly see the attractions of the monastic life. No, I'm not about to undergo a conversion but it was a profound moment and I wanted it to last. Getting back to the bus intent upon the madness of metropolitan Prague, I felt a tinge of regret that I couldn't stay in this place a little longer. We all need these moments to put life's little games into perspective, don't we?

Anyway, that's it for the touring memoirs. I'm signing off. I hope it wasn't like watching someone else's holiday slides. We're going to Anne's sister's again for Christmas on Sunday and staying over for a few days. Whatever I may have said to the contrary, it's always good to be with family.

Our love to Chris, Ellen, Sally, Tina and especially to you Mary, over Christmas 2000. From one old hippy to another... here's wishing you all peace,
Martin.

***

Mary just about made it into the New Year.

***

To Mary and all those who have helped and supported Sgt Pepper's Only Dart Board Band – many thanks. And to four guys who changed our lives and a few more besides – an even bigger thank you:

"If we shadows have offended,
Think but this, and all is mended,
That you have but slumber'd here
While these visions did appear.
And this weak and idle theme,
No more yielding but a dream…"

William Shakespeare

And with a love like that…

Being John Lennon

POPTOMES
an imprint of SAF Publishing

POPTOMES is a new range of music-related literature to compliment the successful rock, jazz and experimental music biographies published under the SAF and FIREFLY imprints.

POPTOMES will take readers on a trip around the peripheries of music culture, often delving into the comic, tragic or just plain bizarre lives of those orbiting planet pop.

The first two POPTOMES are available now:

Industrial Evolution: Through the Eighties with Cabaret Voltaire

Mick Fish's in-depth examination of the renowned Sheffield post-punk Industrial scene and the links to the turbulent corporate culture of the eighties. With The Cabs, Throbbing Gristle, Clock DVA et al.

Being John Lennon: Days in the Life of Sgt Pepper's Only Dart Board Band

Martin Dimery's hilarious first-hand account of trying to maintain a family, a day job and a life, whilst keeping a successful and in-demand Beatles Tribute Band on the road.

Coming later in the year:

AsEverWas: Memoirs of a Beat Survivor

Hammond Guthrie's personal trip through the sixties and seventies via the Acid Tests, Ginsberg, Burroughs, London's UFO Club, Amsterdam's Art elite & the delights of Tangier.

Buy Online

All SAF and Firefly titles are available from the SAF
Publishing website. You can also browse the full range of
rock, pop, jazz and experimental music books we have
available. You can also keep up with our latest releases and
special offers, contact us, and request a catalogue.

www.safpublishing.com

You can also write to us at:
SAF Publishing Ltd, Unit 7, Shaftesbury Centre,
85 Barlby Road, London, W10 6BN. England

Mail Order

All SAF and Firefly titles are also available by mail order from the
world famous Helter Skelter bookshop.
You can phone or fax your order to Helter Skelter on these
numbers:

Telephone: +44 (0)20 7836 1151 or Fax: +44 (0)20 7240 9880
Office hours: Mon-Fri 10:00am–7:00pm,
Sat: 10:00am–6:00pm, Sun: closed.

Helter Skelter Bookshop,
4 Denmark Street, London, WC2H 8LL, United Kingdom.
If you are in London come and visit us, and browse the titles
in person!!

www.safpublishing.com

saf publishing

www.safpublishing.com